In Cod We Trust

Ellef Drægni, ca. 1895

In Cod We Trust

Living the Norwegian Dream

_{Eric}Dregni

University of Minnesota Press
Minneapolis
London

Earlier versions of the chapters in this book were previously published in *The Rake, The Viking,* the *StarTribune,* and *Norway Times.*

Published by the University of Minnesota Press
111 Third Avenue South, Suite 290
Minneapolis, MN 55401-2520
http://www.upress.umn.edu

Library of Congress Cataloging-in-Publication Data

Dregni, Eric, 1968–
　　In cod we trust : living the Norwegian dream / Eric Dregni.
　　　　p.　　cm.
　　"Earlier versions of the chapters in this book were previously published in The Rake, The Viking, the StarTribune, and Norway Times."
　　ISBN 978-0-8166-5623-3 (hc : alk. paper) — ISBN 978-0-8166-5624-0 (pb : alk. paper)
　　1. Norway—Social life and customs—20th century.　2. Norway—Description and travel.　3. Dregni, Eric,—1968—Travel—Norway.　I. Title.
　　DL431.D74　　2008
　　914.8104'5--dc22　　　　　　　　　　　　　　　　　　　　　　2008016682

Printed in the United States of America on acid-free paper

The University of Minnesota is an equal-opportunity educator and employer.

21　20　19　18　17　16　　　　　10　9　8　7　6　5　4

For Eilif and Ellef: it's come full circle.

Contents

A Cambridge Education

I heard the news that I had received a Fulbright Fellowship to Norway the same time I found out my wife, Katy, was pregnant. Scandinavia has always been viewed as a liberal paradise in my family. We had lived in Belgium for a few years when I was little, but my dad extolled the virtues of the Nordic countries that now know how to take care of their people.

A hundred and ten years ago when my great-grandfather Ellef left Norway, the country was overpopulated and many people undernourished. Ellef's brother Johannes came to Minnesota as well but never married, never fit in, and returned home to Norway a failure. I think my dad believes Ellef's journey to America was a mistake all our family's generations since have had to live with.

The lengthy Fulbright application took me weeks of running around to compile the necessary transcripts and recommendations. At the end, I was called in for an interview in front of a panel of five Scandinavian professors and an administrator from the University of Minnesota. On a molded plastic chair that didn't fit my body, I waited outside the room as I heard them laughing and chatting with another student. After fifteen minutes, I heard clapping and cheering inside. A Korean student emerged with a big smile on his face and said *ha det bra*, which I later learned is "good-bye" in Norwegian, to the professors. Obviously, he'd already won the fellowship, so I wondered why I should put myself through an excruciating interview. I didn't know a word of any Scandinavian language apart from the Lord's Prayer my grandfather used to mumble in Norwegian, and that was probably not appropriate. Or was it?

I prepared to bolt, but then I heard a loud "NEXT!" from inside the interrogation room. As I crossed the threshold, five professors and an administrator in business casual attire looked up at me. I was dressed in my dad's old suit and an out-of-fashion red-striped tie. I could feel my whole body sweating as I sat in my suit, which suddenly felt two sizes too small. A distinct smell of camphor emanated from inside the suit, and I pulled a couple of mothballs out of my pocket. I didn't know what to do with them, so I set them on the table as the six judges watched me carefully.

One by one, the professors introduced themselves and their field of interest in Scandinavia. I was too busy trying to swallow to retain any of this information except that the lone man on the panel was interested in Norway. He tilted his forehead forward slightly when he spoke and furrowed his brow so his dark wavy hair came down almost over his eyes. "Eric, we've all had time to review your proposal to study in Trondheim next year," he said. "Your field is creative nonfiction; what are you going to write about?"

"Norway. I'm going to write about Norway," I replied confidently after successfully clearing my throat.

"Well, what about it?" asked a professor whose specialty I believe was Icelandic. She was small but obviously the dominant presence in the room. She took off her glasses impatiently and unbuttoned her cardigan as though she were ready to take me on.

"See, I'm not really sure yet because I haven't had the experience yet. I know that sounds silly, and you probably won't fund something that you don't know what it will be. But I'm going to write about my experiences, the people I meet, rediscovering my family roots. That sort of thing."

The professors absorbed my answer, and some of them slowly took notes on my application. It looked like one of them was doodling little flowery patterns, and the Icelander emphatically underlined something three times that looked like a large "NO."

"Do you speak Norwegian?" the Swedish professor asked politely.

"No, but I did buy a grammar book the other day," I replied. "I think if I know too much about Norway before I go, it'll taint my writing. I want to go over there fresh, you know, with my eyes wide open. My book will be for people who may not know much about Norway but are interested."

"But if you don't speak the language, how will you communicate with the Norwegians?" the Icelandic professor responded.

The Norwegian professor interrupted, "They all speak English perfectly. Actually he doesn't really need to know Norwegian to get by."

Seeing this as an opening to show my good intentions, I interjected, "I do plan on studying Norwegian in Cambridge before going."

The Icelander finally looked impressed and asked, "Will you be at Harvard or MIT?"

"No, no. It's Cambridge, Minnesota, at a little community education class of mostly Scandinavian American farmers." They laughed at the confusion, but I caught two of the professors shaking their heads sadly.

The Norwegian professor asked, "You wrote in your application that you have distant relatives in Norway from the Lusterfjord at the end of the Sognefjord. What part of the fjord are they from?"

Before I could embarrass myself with my lack of geographical knowledge, the Icelandic professor interrupted, "Oh, you Norwegians! All you want to talk about is your fjords. What does it matter where on the fjord his relatives are from?"

"But everyone knows everyone on the Sognefjord," he explained. "It's possible I've been to the town. This is the longest fjord in Norway and is a very important place." I realized I had an ally on the panel as the Icelandic professor shook her head and muttered the words "damn fjords."

To head off an inter-Scandinavian feud, I said, "Part of the adventure of my year will be to find my family's roots and why they left Norway. I want to discover how the country has changed over the past hundred years and how people live now. In the U.S., we have preconceived notions about Norway, and I want to see what is true."

"You know that the university in Trondheim, NTNU, is a technology school, right?" the Swedish professor asked.

"Yes, of course," I lied confidently. I started to blush as they waited for a better response. After an uncomfortable pause, I added, "They do have an English department, though, so I plan on working with some of the professors there."

"You already speak English, and the department is mostly to help Norwegians master the language," one of the professors pointed out.

"Which is exactly why I'll fit right in," I replied boldly. "I can help them with their language skills."

The Icelandic professor had had enough. She put her glasses on only to take them off again for added emphasis. "OK, let me get this straight. You don't know Norwegian, you want to study writing at a science and technology university, and you don't even know what you're going to write about."

"That's correct," I replied, happy that I finally knew the answer to one of her questions. She sat back contentedly as though she'd won her argument and cleared up any confusion about my eligibility.

"It sounds like an interesting project," the Norwegian professor added hopefully. He then gave a little smirk toward the Icelandic professor. "I suppose," he said, "you'll include this interview in your book if you get the fellowship."

When I arrived home, I told Katy about the disastrous interview. "Don't get your hopes up for a year in Norway," I said and described the scene in the stuffy little room full of professors looking for flaws in my proposal. Then I noticed that she was just sitting in a chair staring at a little piece of white plastic. "Are you OK?" I asked.

"There are two lines," she said without looking up.

"What? Two lines of what?"

"Just two lines. Don't worry about your interview because we have something bigger on our plate." She held up the piece of plastic for me to see two faint red lines on a paper insert. "I'm pregnant."

I quickly sat down. "Wow! That's great." Katy had gone off the pill three weeks earlier because our doctor had told us that sometimes couples in their early thirties take years to get pregnant. She patted her slender belly in anticipation.

Over the next month, we reminded ourselves that we were going to have a baby. We plotted out the due date to the end of October; we bought some baby clothes and got used to the idea of changing hundreds of pungent diapers.

Just when we were beginning to envision our future life as new parents, the phone rang. I recognized the voice as the woman from the scholarship office. "I have some good news! You've been awarded the Fulbright Fellowship to Trondheim. Congratulations!"

When I hung up the phone, I remembered that I couldn't accept the prize because the baby was due when we'd be in Norway. Katy watched me and asked, "Who was that? Why are you so pale?"

"Do you remember when you said that it would be great to go to Norway?" She nodded. "Well, I got the fellowship that will pay for both of us to live there for a year."

"Oh my goodness, really? You have to take it!" she said.

"What about the baby?" I asked, surprised that she still wanted to go.

She paused, then said, "They have hospitals in Norway, don't they?"

I looked through the pamphlets about the Fulbright Fellowship to confirm that both of us were covered under the insurance plan. One brochure asserted that this was some of the best health care insurance around because Fulbright comes under the auspices of the U.S. State Department. Deep in the documentation, however, I discovered the clause: "Spouses of grantees will be covered . . . except under conditions of pregnancy."

Now we were worried. I called up Blue Cross/Blue Shield, but they wouldn't cover birth abroad. Katy called up other insurers in search of coverage. Pregnancy is considered a "pre-existing condition," as if it's some sort of disease, and no one would have us.

"You will probably be eligible to be covered by the Norwegian system. Why don't you call up the consulate?" the woman at the scholarship office said. I rang the Norwegian consulate in downtown Minneapolis, and they were painfully vague. I supposed they didn't want herds of pregnant Americans arriving on their shores looking for free health care.

I called the center for international students in Trondheim to ask if we'd be covered by the national Norwegian system.

"I don't see why not," the woman with a lilting Norwegian accent responded.

I asked if she could send us the proper forms.

"There's really no rush; you can just fill them out once you arrive," she said in a relaxed tone.

I asked her to send me copies so I could get a jump start and fax them right back.

"You'll need to file the documents with the government once you get here, anyway, so you don't need to send them back. Besides, almost everyone is on vacation over the summer."

I'd already been to Norway, when I was four years old. My only souvenir of that trip is a family photo with me covered in manure. My family went to visit the Drægni farm in the town of Fortun that some of our relatives called home. While my parents discovered the headstones in the graveyard where our great-great-grandparents were buried, my two older brothers and I were already using the tombstones as shields so we could play "war."

This was my dad's pilgrimage to find the hometown of his grandfather Ellef. Now he was seeing the tombstones of Ellef's parents, graves that hadn't been seen by anyone in our family for generations. Ellef left Norway in 1893 at the age of eighteen and didn't return. He never saw his parents again.

"Aaarrrggh! You shot me!" I screamed to my brothers and feigned a dramatic death on the green grass of the cemetery. My older brothers stood proudly over my limp body.

People in town who had faced occupation by the Germans thirty years before were not amused. After one too many imaginary gunfights, my parents yanked us out of the graveyard to go visit some distant family members. We were supposed to be on our best behavior to show how respectable the American relatives can be.

We sandwiched ourselves into the little rental car, and my dad drove to the house of his great-uncle and great-aunt, Ola and Lina Drægni. An older man and woman with these storybook names opened the door; they spoke only Norwegian. Ola and Lina invited us inside once they understood that we were family from America. Lina served open-faced sandwiches and lemonade, while Ola put his fingers to his forehead and pranced around the room to amaze us kids with how he killed the giant elk that was now mounted on the wall. Not a word of English was needed.

During this meeting of Old and New Worlds at the doorstep of their house, I continued our game of "war" in the yard and fell in an enormous manure heap. My brothers were bent over laughing as our polite Norwegian relatives cleaned the excrement off my overalls. My brothers' laughter ceased when they realized they'd have to spend the rest of the trip confined in the car with their smelly brother. My dad cut short the visit to his great-uncle and great-aunt, but not before he had quickly snapped a picture of all of us together.

Katy and I were going to spend a year in a country where we didn't know anyone and didn't speak the language. How would we buy groceries? How would we get around town? How would we do anything? The Norwegian on the fellowship committee claimed that we could get by speaking English, and nonchalantly assured us that we would have no problems—almost as though going to Norway is like moving to the suburbs.

The drive to our class in Cambridge, Minnesota, took one hour each way after dark to a cinderblock building on the edge of town. The coffeepot sputtered the last of the water through the grounds when we walked through the door of our classroom. A red-and-white checkered tablecloth was placed carefully under the Styrofoam cups, coffeepot, and plate of cookies. Ornate hand-painted wooden boards were tacked up on the white cement walls next to children's construction paper artwork. Before class had even begun, it was time for a break. "Hi, everybody," our teacher, Carla, said. "It looks like Wes has made some fresh apple pie and some chocolate chip cookies."

"Oh, I just had a little time before class to put together a pie," Wes blushed. "I'm from Braham, you know, the pie capital of Minnesota."

On the whiteboard, Carla wrote in Norwegian: "What is your name?" and "Where do you live?" Then she said, "Now let's go around and ask each other."

Katy was first. She turned to the middle-aged woman next to her and successfully asked her name. Katy stumbled over the difficult vowels of the next question: "*Hvor bor du?*" She pointed at the woman but only managed to stutter, "*Hor... Hor...*"

The woman looked at her wide-eyed, and Katy finally finished the question. I fidgeted in my seat, worried we were going to get kicked out of Norwegian class, but Katy charmed the class with her embarrassed giggle, and everyone laughed along.

"Maybe it's best if we introduce ourselves first in English," Carla said.

I couldn't remember anyone's names, and it didn't help that the people in the class introduced themselves between bites of pie and sips of coffee with powdered cream whitener.

The class's attention then turned to us, the obvious new-comers. "We're moving to Trondheim for a year," I said. The class let out an excited, "Oh!"

Katy added, "And I'm going to have a baby there!"

"Oh my goodness," said Carla. "We better get down to business."

The pie was set aside, the caffeine kicked in, and the whole class chipped in with advice. Norm, a quiet man who sat with his hands together over his stomach, said that he had lived in Trondheim for a year in the 1960s. Out of his bag, he pulled a detailed map of the town and a pile of books on Norway to lend us. "If you get invited over to someone's house in Trondheim, dinner will usually be cod, boiled potatoes, and peas or something like that. In other words, they eat pretty much the same food as we do," he told us.

The woman whom Katy had called a whore said, "If the Norwegians start correcting you all the time when you speak, I learned the perfect phrase, 'I'm sorry, I'm not as smart as you are.'" Now we could be passive-aggressive in both English and Norwegian.

Katy declared, "We're leaving in a matter of months, and we don't even have a place to live." She pulled out a list of apartment ads downloaded from the Internet. Carla and Wes helped translate the listings as Norm opened a map to point out the prettiest areas to live in Trondheim.

Carla then led a Norwegian vocabulary lesson for childbirth. Brianna, a twelve-year-old, looked both disgusted and fascinated, but at least her attention had shifted from wanting to shoot deer.

After learning the anatomical and intimate words for birth, it was time for another snack break before going home. "How about I bring treats next week?" I asked at the end of the lesson, thinking that I'd bring something typically Norwegian. "Are pickled herring and smoked salmon OK?"

"Oh yuck! You actually eat that stuff?" Brianna asked.

The others looked around nervously, perhaps worried they'd have to eat herring to be polite. Wes came to their rescue by assuring everyone that he'd make treats for the next lesson. In fact, he'd already started his Christmas caramels. "I've used 70 liters of cream, 90 liters of corn syrup, and 120 kilos of sugar," he said. "I'm almost out of sugar, though, so I might have to go back to the store for more."

Thanks to our first class, we had found an apartment and got stacks of books to read, and everyone left with a ziplock bag full of chocolate chip cookies. Most important, Wes gave us the address of friends of friends named Knut and Inger who live in Trondheim, and helped us write letters to introduce ourselves. We'd made first contact.

From Colony to Homeland

I told Katy that she should ask the stewardess if there were any bulkhead seats available for us since she was pregnant. Once Katy posed the question, the Icelandair stewardess rushed to find an empty business class seat for her so she could stretch her legs. Only one seat was free, though, so I stayed wedged between two people on the packed flight to Oslo.

I kept my elbows from nudging my neighbors as they ate their airline meal. In between bites of what tasted vaguely like chicken, an older Norwegian man next to me asked where I came from.

"Minnesota? Oh, you mean the other Norway!" he exclaimed. "Are you going to visit family in Norway?"

"My great-grandfather came from the Sognefjord area, but I only have an address of some distant cousins," I told him.

"I'm sure they will be very happy that you have come back," he said.

I explained that I was born in the U.S., so I'm actually fourth-generation. I'd only been to Norway once when I was four and fell in a dung heap.

He wasn't sure how to react but finally said, "Still, I'm sure your relatives will be glad to have you back home in Norway." I was perplexed that he didn't understand that I'm not Norwegian.

On the other side of me, a young woman wearing a "Hard Rock Café: Chicago" T-shirt pulled off her headphones, which continued to squeal hip-hop. "Minnesota? I just got done working as a counselor at a Norwegian camp in northern Minnesota," she said. "I can't believe how you view us Norwegians."

"What do you mean?" I asked.

"Your idea of Norway is stuck back a hundred years. You think we all sit around and knit. When we don't knit, you think we dance around in *bunads*."

"A *bunad*? What's that?" I asked.

"You don't know? It's our national costume, a hand-stitched traditional dress. Each region has its own pattern," she said proudly. "I even met a lot of older people in Minnesota who have them."

The man and the young woman began a lively exchange in Norwegian. Although I couldn't understand most of what they said, I knew they contradicted each other politely about Minnesota.

The conversation hit a lull, when we spotted the stewardess wheeling her beverage cart down the narrow aisle. She asked the Norwegian couple in front of us, "Would you like an after-dinner beverage?" The man pulled out the list of drinks they wanted; the stewardess had to scurry back to the galley to replenish her supply. When the next group saw how much free liquor the other passengers were served, a young blond man asked, "Can we get the same thing they got?"

The exasperated stewardess replied, "I know that liquor is expensive in Norway, but take it easy!" She then made an announcement: each person could get only two drinks. "OK, that's fair," the blond Norwegian man with the long list continued. "Can I get two double Scotches?" The waitress explained that two doubles is the same as four drinks but gave him the whisky anyway to avoid complaints against the airline's liquor policy.

A woman in her seventies wearing a rain bonnet with plastic daisies gave her drink order half in Norwegian, half in broken English. The stewardess advised her, "You probably don't want to have both a screwdriver and a Baileys." The older woman cupped her ear, so the stewardess raised her voice. "You know orange juice and milk don't mix well in your stomach, and we will have some turbulence when we go over the mountains." The flower-capped woman wiggled her index finger, either because she didn't understand or because this advice was nonsense. The stewardess served the beverages and double-checked in the pouch in front of the woman's seat to make sure there was a barf bag.

When I didn't ask for a drink, my two seatmates looked at me in disbelief. I explained that the alcohol combined with the jet lag would make me too tired. Besides, I didn't think it was fair that I drink while Katy, who got a plush seat in business class because she was pregnant, couldn't indulge.

The older man next to me nodded his head thoughtfully as though to compliment me on being responsible or perhaps because he didn't believe my story. Then he whispered, "I was going to ask the stewardess for your drinks, too."

After the beverage cart disappeared, conversations got louder for a time and then died down. I understood why the stewardess had been so generous with the liquor, when most of the passengers eventually snoozed off their drinks for the rest of the flight.

I couldn't sleep, as I realized that the next time we'd be in Minnesota, we'd have a baby. And what about our year in Norway? Would the Norwegians speak English or understand our garbled words of their language? How would we survive the dark, cold winter?

With these questions filing through my head, I reassured myself that we could always turn around and go home if need be. If we did, though, the fellowship might require a reimbursement of the money they'd spent on us. In other words, we had to stick it out.

Out the oval airplane window, I saw the sun rise through a red curtain of clouds as we made landfall. The mountains of western Norway plunged into the sea, and the updrafts shook the plane. Luckily, the woman filled with Baileys Irish Cream and vodka and orange juice was snoring happily.

We crossed southern Norway and touched down in Oslo. On the gangway, I saw Katy chatting with a handsome, well-dressed man from business class. She introduced us and told me, "He's a diplomat at the Norwegian embassy in Washington and has been giving me all sorts of advice about living here." "I'm surprised you're going to Trondheim for a year. Usually visitors only go to Oslo or stay in the fjords around Bergen." Waving good-bye, he said, "Welcome to our funny little country."

A Beautiful Day in Hell

From the window of the cab, Katy pointed out the sign for the town of "Hell" as we passed through on this balmy eighty-degree day in mid-July. The name inevitably gets chuckles from photo-snapping English-speakers: "Go to ...," "A cold day in ...," "Welcome to ...," etc. The name doesn't do the area justice, with the tidy farms and gently sloping mountains overlooking the chilly waters where a large Nazi battleship supposedly lies sunk at the bottom—perhaps along with the spirit of Quisling haunting Hell.

We had just landed at the Trondheim airport an hour away from downtown, so the taxi driver took us through Hell to the center of Trondheim. The dominant structure in town is Nidarosdomen cathedral with spires that have poked the sky since its construction in 1070. Gargoyles jut out from the eaves with tortured grimaces, and the church's facade has a lineup of apostles and saints, some carrying a basket of the skulls of beheaded monks. Somewhere under the church—no one is sure where—the holy bones of Saint Olav were supposedly buried after his defeat at nearby Stiklestad in 1030.

The driver circled the roundabout in the exact center of town marked by an enormous sundial with a statue of the founder of Trondheim, evangelical Olav Tryggvason, offering people the choice of converting to Christianity or dying by his sharp sword. The words of these Viking kings were not idle banter, as shown on the little "Monk's Island," Munkholmen, which we could see across the bay from Trondheim, where Vikings impaled decapitated heads on stakes to ward off visitors.

We entered our neighborhood, Lademoen, which is bordered by the enormous German U-boat factory, DORA. Postwar, the factory with its five-meter-thick walls, was deemed impossible to blow up, so it was turned into a enormous concrete bowling alley. Dockworkers can now bowl and tip back a Dahl's pilsner from the local brewery on the other site of our new neighborhood.

Katy pointed out the brightly painted art nouveau buildings that stood at least four stories tall. I liked the crooked wooden houses with rust-free Volvo Amazons from the 1960s parked on the cobblestone streets. I asked the cabbie if this was the most luxurious area in town. "Oh no, this is one of the poorest areas in Trondheim," he said.

He pulled over the cab on our new street with a sweeping view of a giant cemetery. "Oh, it can't be that," Katy said, pointing to the only building it could be. "That must be some sort of military barracks." The nondescript white cement apartment building stood three stories tall and ran the whole block. No trees were planted along the sidewalk, and cars puffed exhaust up the walls of the cold building.

We double-checked the address as the cab driver unloaded our eight bags onto the asphalt parking lot in back. I gasped at the expensive cab fare of $75, and we sat on our suitcases and looked at the white cement monstrosity that would be our new home. "What are we doing here?" asked Katy. We had both been suckered in by tourist posters and guidebooks of quaint Norwegian cabins with grass roofs overlooking the fjords, but here we were waiting for our new landlord to let us into the concrete flat that cost more than half of our monthly stipend from Fulbright. Katy patted her belly with our baby incubating inside, and I could tell she was worried.

"I'm sure it's all going to be fine," I said unconvincingly as we sat on our bags, waiting for our landlord, Arne, and contemplating our fate.

After a half hour, Arne pulled up in his fancy maroon Renault and excused himself repeatedly for being late. His spunky personality and full head of blond hair made him seem younger than his fifty years of age. The apartment belonged to his son

Trond, who lived in southern Norway. "This is Trond's home, like Trondheim, which means Trond's home," he explained laughing, but corrected us that Trondheim literally means "home of the Trøndere people."

I don't know whether it was Arne's joking personality or because the apartment was much nicer from the inside. In any case, our moods were lifted by seeing a friendly face to help us get settled. Our small one-bedroom apartment incorporated Scandinavian minimalist design with large windows, a glass door leading to a balcony, heated tile floors in the bathroom, and a large metal woodstove.

I asked Arne why the windows had no screens to keep out the bugs. "Oh, we do have mosquitoes here," he replied, "but they don't come out until after dark." I pointed out that it didn't really get dark in the summer.

"Well, once the sun goes down, they come out." Sunset, we learned, wasn't until about 2 a.m., and even then we never saw bugs. A reprieve from the clouds of Minnesota mosquitoes that loomed over our heads back home.

Arne just laughed and said that Norway still has some problems. "For example, if you have bicycles, you best keep them locked. Even Norwegians have learned to steal."

The apartment was furnished, but Arne looked around, unsatisfied with the furniture that his son Trond had left. Katy and I thought everything looked fine, but Arne took one look at the bedding and pronounced, "It just won't do." His wife, Oddbjørg, would bring new sheets and duvet covers. Everyone gets his or her own quilt in Norway, probably so your partner can't steal the covers—not a bad idea at all. "Tomorrow," he said, "we shall go to IKEA to buy you things for your apartment."

"Screw Yourself" at IKEA

"See that? Those are the Swedish colors: yellow and blue. That is very bad. Very bad for Norway," Arne joked, while we pulled up at the giant IKEA box store in Trondheim. We had never been in an IKEA store before, but we had asked Arne to bring us there so we could buy a table and chair. Arne agreed happily but made it clear he did not approve of the quality of this Swedish chain. "We don't shop here," he said. "It's mostly just for students or people who are newly divorced."

Saturdays at IKEA are a mad rush of bargain hunters grabbing for cheap household decorations, like Viking berserkers in search of British plunder. A bus stop was next to the entrance, and shoppers jammed bookshelves, packaged desks, and other furniture through the tiny doors of the city bus. Most passengers getting off the bus headed right to the IKEA cafeteria for their famous fatty meatballs. The Norwegian IKEA stores sell fifty thousand meatballs a week, and the newspapers reported that only one man in the whole country knows the secret recipe. Perhaps the Swedish company didn't trust the dissemination of this classified information to any Norwegian, who might leak it to the general public. Hungry diners love them even though they have no idea what's inside.

We survived the chaos of the hungry shoppers and found a nice table and chair. As Arne drove us back to the apartment, we saw the new IKEA print ads on bus stops throughout town that featured cool teens with blank, drugged-out expressions. Scribbled prominently above the yellow IKEA logo on all the posters was the phrase "Screw Yourself" in English. Katy and I were suddenly wary of IKEA's furniture and realized that Arne might be right.

At first I thought this "Screw Yourself" graffiti must be the work of witty Norse taggers spray-painting their opposition to this corporate giant from next-door Sweden. Upon closer inspection, I noticed perfectly consistent writing over each poster of the dazed hipsters in uncomfortable poses on the wooden furniture. This was IKEA warning its own customers of the perils of its wares.

When we got home from the store with our new furniture, I rang up IKEA to ask if they understood what their ad campaign meant for English speakers. The IKEA customer service representative responded calmly in perfect English, "We've had many complaints about that. What we meant by that was 'build it yourself.' I don't think that the advertisers understood the other meaning when they made the posters."

A Norwegian friend didn't buy it. "Oh, they knew what they were doing. They wanted to appeal to a younger audience, so they used American slang." Even so, I was surprised by this bizarre double—or triple—entendre. The Norwegians could appropriate the crassest of American culture and somehow strip it of offensiveness just to make it fun. Some countries, like France, for instance, worry about U.S. cultural imperialism dominating their own, but IKEA's slogan was an example of clever Norwegians choosing from the smorgasbord of American pop culture to spoof our slang.

IKEA's line that it was a simple mistranslation also seemed odd because the word *skrue* (screw) in Norwegian can mean "crazy old kook," as used for the translation of Disney's Uncle Scrooge *(Onkel Skrue)*. What company would want to associate itself with that miserly penny-pincher?

I called the customer service representative in Oslo to find out if they'd use the same campaign in the U.K. and U.S. to attract, or distract, customers. "IKEA has only made these posters in Norway," she told me, but added that IKEA will keep up its "Screw Yourself" advertising blitz across Norway.

Janteloven

We'd seen our neighbor out on his balcony: a quiet, older man who lived alone. Late one Saturday morning, we knocked on his door and waited patiently while he grasped for the doorknob. The door squeaked open, and the man propped it open just enough to peek his head out.

Katy gave a dimpled smile and began speaking in her disarming voice. She'd worked out a little introduction in Norwegian complete with an excuse as to why we were bothering him. "Hello, we just moved in next door; you probably heard us."

No response from him.

She continued with friendly gusto, "We come from the U.S. and I'm five months pregnant. I'll have the baby in Norway."

Still silence.

"We wondered if we could borrow a hammer and screwdriver to put up a picture."

He looked at us. Paused. He brushed back his gray hair, adjusted his shirt uncomfortably with his right hand, and scratched his head. "*Nei,*" he said and slowly shut the door. We stood in the hallway perplexed and amazed. Had we done something wrong?

We had a similar situation with our young neighbor—probably a student—who lived below us. Whenever we passed him in the hall, we said "Hi," but he ignored us each time. In fact, he wouldn't even look at us.

When we went on walks, people would stare at us as we approached them on the sidewalk. Because they looked at us so intently, we greeted them with a simple "Hello" or "*God morgen*" once we were close. They instantly looked away, embarrassed, as if we had just asked for cash or mooned them. Norwegians on the street usually noticed Katy's pregnant belly, then some-

20

times looked over at me with an approving smile as though to say, "Good job!" Even then, they wouldn't return a greeting. All we could deduce was that *we* were the ones being rude and breaking some sacred rule.

Then we met Knut and Inger, friends of Wes from Norwegian class. Inger was pregnant, so she and Katy hit it off right away. Knut and Inger's baby was due a couple of months after ours. They had recently moved to Trondheim from western Norway and had worked in the Sognefjord, where my great-grandfather Ellef was born. Inger, a librarian, worked on a book boat that traveled up and down the fjord to tiny towns of just a few people to bring them something to read. "They would check out books in the spring, and we'd return in the fall. It was exciting to see the kids growing up six months later," she told us in English. "I'd stay on the boat for about six weeks at a time."

"No one lives there really," Knut said. He told how he felt so removed from civilization living in Sognefjord. "It was terrible; all anyone wanted to talk about was hunting." I thought of Ola Drægni putting his hands on his forehead to show how he brought down an enormous elk. Knut added, though, that he did enjoy shooting moose and that we would have to come over for moose steaks some time.

In spite of his fondness for hunting, Knut Bull wore dapper tweed suits and silk ties, which gave him a professorial look that fit in with his job as curator of a museum in Trondheim. He thoughtfully smoked a pipe to complete the look. His great-great-uncle was the famous violin virtuoso Ole Bull, who encouraged thousands of Norwegians, and possibly my great-grandfather Ellef, to seek greener pastures in the American Midwest.

Knut was opening up a new world to me with his insight into Norwegian culture. I explained the cold behavior of our neighbors, and he wasn't surprised. "You must know about *Janteloven*," he advised. "This is the law of Jante and is why people seem so shy. They don't want to show they are better

than you." I failed to see the connection between greeting a
neighbor and encouraging a superiority complex until he told
me that Jante is a fictional Norwegian town from the 1933
book *En flyktning krysser sitt spor (A Fugitive Crosses His Tracks)*
by Axel Sandemose. The rigid social laws of Jante keep the
people subdued.

Knut showed me a copy of the book, and I read: "You who
have grown up elsewhere can never fully appreciate the inevit-
ability of the Jante Law. You will find it funny and will never
know its deadly oppression of a working-class youth in Jante.
With the ten Jante Rules . . . Jante holds its people down":

1. You shall not believe that you are something.
2. You shall not believe that you are equal to anyone else.
3. You shall not believe that you are wiser than others.
4. You shall not imagine yourself better than your
   neighbor.
5. You shall not believe that you know more than we do.
6. You shall not believe that you can rise above others.
7. You shall not believe that you are capable.
8. You shall not laugh at anyone else.
9. You shall not believe that anyone cares about you.
10. You shall not believe that you can teach us anything.

I took *Janteloven* to be a joke, a satire of little towns everywhere. The author Sandemose must have been bitter about his
small-minded town that didn't understand him. Perhaps his
town of Jante was like Sinclair Lewis's backbiting town of Go-
pher Prairie in *Main Street* or Garrison Keillor's Lake Wobegon.

Nevertheless, I often heard Norwegians referring to *Janteloven* as synonymous with being humble, and therefore a posi-
tive attribute that had led to this egalitarian-minded society.
Politicians weren't afraid to conjure up *Janteloven* to promote
their policies of sharing the country's — and everyone's —
wealth with those less fortunate. Equality at all costs. On Norwegian radio, I heard a DJ explaining the origin of the Jante

laws to a listener who had always been told by her parents, "Just remember to follow the *Janteloven*."

The Norwegian *Janteloven* struck me as a thinly disguised encouragement of conformity, yet this fictitious law also banned vain braggarts. Since most Norwegians seem to subconsciously follow *Janteloven*, the result is a people who are modest, unassuming, shy, and often have a funny, self-effacing sense of humor. These ten commandments may have begun as a morality tale of how not to act, but over time these rules were adopted to teach kids not to be self-important narcissists.

Knut confirmed that "Sandemose meant *Janteloven* to be ironic, but unfortunately it's often very true. The problem is in job interviews when we don't try to sell ourselves like you Americans do." I could imagine that to obey the *Janteloven*, résumés probably remained rather sparse. If I looked for a job in Norway, I'd better be careful not to talk up my accomplishments too much or I'd look like I'm bragging. But how do employers know what you've done?

One of my professors in Trondheim, an American, told me a Norwegian saying, "'Don't go tramping in the salad,' which means 'don't open your mouth to show how dumb you are.' I've found that Norwegians are very careful not to offend people." I told him about our neighbor closing the door on us, and the professor was shocked that someone decided to take the law of Jante into his own hands, as though the neighbor were a social vigilante preventing anyone from being outgoing.

A Norwegian professor told me that "in Norway, people don't ask, 'What do you do?' like you Americans, because work isn't our life. Instead, we ask 'Where are you from?'"

Katy and I slowly learned how to properly strike up a conversation in our newly adopted town of Trondheim. We began with the fact that we're from Minnesota, which the Norwegians refer to as "our colony in America"—then we were asked if we knew their relatives in Red Wing or Richfield. Sometimes they even suggested we could look up their second cousin twice removed when we got back.

Once the ice was broken further—after the commentary on the weather—we found Norwegians to be grudgingly warm, like a glacier thawing into a slow-moving mountain stream. The challenge was to chip away at these layers of ice, as we found with the neighbors in our apartment building.

Our neighbors did become friendlier—with time. We subdued our greetings so as not to frighten them, and they furrowed their brows with a forced acknowledging smile when we passed. Our neighbor who refused to lend us tools soon nodded a pleasant "*God dag*" and would almost grin when he saw us. Luckily, Katy and I had each other to talk to as we wondered if we'd made a mistake in coming to this cold country. We could always return to Minnesota if our hosts didn't warm up as the impending winter cooled us. We hoped that by the time the snow flew in Trondheim, we'd progress beyond the small talk about the weather.

The young neighbor downstairs still would pay no attention to us. One day, though, we saw him communicating in sign language with his roommate. Of course! He was deaf. Still, it was a mystery why he wouldn't look at us.

Another tenant in our building hailed from Tromsø, in the far north of Norway, and wanted me to come bowling in the old German U-boat bunker. Whenever we would meet in the stairwell, he would greet me enthusiastically. His animated voice continued when he asked how I was doing. Then the conversation died. I struggled to keep up a discussion about the weather or any other safe topic, but he'd just purse his lips, look at the ground, and nod slowly.

This was why Katy and I were relieved to gather with Knut and Inger every Saturday at a café in Trondheim next to an art gallery with some of their friends, who didn't seem to obey the rules of *Janteloven*.

Knut's friend Leif explained that he was from Sweden and didn't believe that Norwegians were unfriendly, just reserved. Even so, he wanted to break this mold. "When I moved into my new apartment a few years ago, I thought that I should be like you Americans," he said, clutching his fist with conviction. "Rather than waiting years to ever meet or speak with my neighbors, I'd just knock on their door and introduce myself."

After a pause I asked, "Well, what happened?"

"Oh, I'm still thinking about it," he replied as he rubbed his chin. "See, if I did ring their doorbell and told them I just moved in, they'd probably look at me and say, 'So?'"

The Chest

As we unpacked our bags in our new apartment, I discovered that my dad had put in some yellowed documents that belonged to my great-grandfather Ellef. These old papers had been stored in a crude wooden chest that Ellef hauled over from Norway, which sat in a corner of our living room in Minnesota as a reminder of our link to Norway. The leather handles of the chest had dried out, the luster of the dark red milk paint was faded, but a varnished emblem of "Halifax" had resisted time and was indelibly attached to the side. Other relatives from Sweden had brought ornate chests with art deco latches and silk interiors, but Ellef's Norwegian chest was a simple wooden box with iron clasps and hinges. He probably hammered the metalwork himself on his anvil. For years, I viewed the chunky chest as just another piece of furniture to set a sweating glass of Kool-Aid on, and I got in trouble for leaving a ring on this family heirloom. Later, we used the chest as a stand for our 1980s-era Magnavox television.

Ellef's documents were tucked inside and assured he wouldn't be turned away on arrival in the New World in 1893. Unless the customs agents spoke Norwegian, the documents stood little chance of being understood when he docked at Halifax, Canada.

Ellef's parson wrote one document to vouch for Ellef as a good Christian and a well-behaved gentleman who wasn't skipping out on a wife back home in Norway:

> Ellef of parents lofter houseman Ole Ellefsen Drægni and wife Karen J. is according to Lysters parsonages churchbook born 19 June 1875, christened, confirmed, etc. About his behavior there, is as far as it is known, nothing detrimental. He is not bound with public marriage promise. He leaves

now, for Amerika beckons wherefore he is taken off the records of this congregation. Lyster the 14th April 1893. N. Daal, Priest and parson. Legal payment one krone 00/ore.

The other document used a different spelling of his first name, which he changed frequently, and claimed he had a clean record of health:

Ellif born in Fortun of parents Ole Ellefsen Drægni and Karen Johannesdatter and living in Fortun, seven years old has been given injections against measles by the under-signed in 1882, the 22nd of August. By close observation between the 7th and 9th day after injection, I have found all the signs that show them to be genuine measles; they were whole and not destroyed filled with a clear fluid, depressed at the center, and surrounded by a red circle.

In the 1800s, leprosy was still a serious disease — the city of Bergen alone had three leper colonies. My great-grandfather Ellef was healthy enough not to become infected with the bac-teria while he prepared to board ship in Bergen.

Ellef left Norway in 1893, and the situation in the United States was improving, or at least that's what the flamboyant Norwegian violin virtuoso Ole Bull and other land developers promised with visions of a "New Norway." The Civil War was over, and there were renewed promises of prosperity. The Dakota War of 1862 in Minnesota still worried immigrants, even though the U.S. military had squashed the Native Ameri-cans with a mass hanging in Mankato and the Indians once again lost more land. The Homestead Act of 1862 opened much of the land for new immigrants to settle even farther west. Ellef read postcards from family who had settled in Wisconsin and Minnesota and assured their kin back home that life in Amer-ica offered many opportunities. These new Norwegian arrivals in the Midwest promised Ellef a bed to sleep in until he found a job.

We inherited Ellef's chest because my father's father, Al, didn't want his father's (Ellef's) old stuff from the Old Coun-try cluttering up his living room in south Minneapolis. In fact, my grandfather never spoke to me about his father's journey from Norway. I discovered that my grandfather spoke only Norwegian (with Swedish mixed in) until he was six years old and started school. When I was little, he only spoke it when pressed to say his Norwegian blessing before dinner or when he and my grandma didn't want the kids to understand.

My grandfather Al played down his Norwegian roots to better adapt to life in America. "In America, you should speak English," he told me when I was eight. He was very proud to live in the United States and gave me a lesson in how to properly raise, lower, and fold the Stars and Stripes. I took one end of the enormous banner, and my grandpa the other to fold the flag respectfully into a triangle. A corner of the cloth brushed the tall grass. I listened as my grandfather scolded me, "Never let the flag touch the ground, or you have to burn it!" He then smiled and said that it would be our secret.

My grandfather often told us the story of how he had tried to fight in World War I, but the day he became old enough to join the army was Armistice Day, November 11, 1918. I later learned that the loyalty of Nordic immigrants was questioned by the U.S. authorities because of the historical connections with Germany or their left-wing activities as organizers of unions and co-ops. Kaiser Wilhelm vacationed in Norway, loved the Norse sagas, and even erected Viking statues in the Sognefjord near my ancestors' home. Any language that sounded remotely like German was viewed with suspicion during the World Wars. Norwegian immigrants learned English in a hurry.

Because my great-grandfather Ellef was a self-sufficient skilled blacksmith, my grandfather Al could afford to go to Minnesota College of Law (later William Mitchell College of Law) and become the youngest lawyer in the state because an undergraduate degree wasn't required. In one generation, the family breadwinner shifted from poverty to prosperity, from blue collar to white.

I remember as a teenager watching the evening news one day with my grandfather when he complained about groups of Vietnamese arriving in the United States. "All these new immigrants are ruining it for us native Americans," he muttered. I pointed out that his father, Ellef, probably met the same criticism when he came over with all his belongings in his big wooden chest. My grandfather listened carefully to me but kept his skeptical view of these new arrivals.

My dad revived (or reinvented) Old World customs that were purposely ignored by my grandfather. He began with "Norwegian dinner," a bimonthly excuse to espouse our glorious Norwegian roots to his captive family.

Considering that Norway is a country with a culinary delicacy of fish soaked in lye, we weren't thrilled by my dad's newfound enthusiasm. He made a special trip to Ingebretsen's Scandinavian market in south Minneapolis to shop for food that most grocery stores deemed unfit for human consumption. My dad lovingly set the table with a blue-and-red printed tablecloth, candles, and wooden knives and breadboards he had bought in Norway. But the mood lighting still couldn't hide the food: boiled potatoes, cauliflower, and some sort of bland white fish were covered with an even blander white sauce, all on a white plate. Pickled herring added the only flavor to the meal.

"So this is why there are no Scandinavian restaurants in the Twin Cities. Now I know why people in Norway always went hungry!" my brother John joked.

"How did grandpa get out of this dinner?" asked my other brother, Michael. "He's the most Norwegian of all of us!"

I just thought how lucky we were to be in America and not have to eat like this every day.

My mom proudly declared that she had no Scandinavian relatives—a rarity in Minnesota—and therefore didn't have to eat Norwegian dinner. Perhaps blinded by his Scandinavian evangelism, my dad couldn't understand her reluctance about such a delicious meal. My mom had a giant genealogical chart that proved her pure Anglo blue blood all the way back to the Middle Ages. My dad inspected the chart carefully and discovered William the Conqueror, the Norman who invaded England in 1066. During Norwegian dinner, we paged through a book on Vikings and discovered that William the Conqueror was the great-great-great-grandson of Viking Rollo the Grandeur, who was less than five feet tall and so fat he rode a mule. Rollo was kicked out of Norway, then Denmark, and finally settled in Normandy. When convenient, Rollo broke his alliance with the French king and went on rampages through northern France. His real name was Hrolf, but perhaps his rotund belly earned him the nickname of "Rollo," which he couldn't shake even after assuming the title of "Duke of Normandy."

All this meant that my dad was vindicated when he debunked her Scandinavian-free claim, and my mom had to eat Norwegian dinner. She grimaced as her white plate was loaded up with the bland creamy fish and potatoes. She was rediscovering her roots.

Once I turned eighteen, my dad succeeded in keeping us at the table thanks to a small shot of eighty-proof aquavit and a beer chaser. Norwegian sailors discovered that when they stored their aquavit in old sherry barrels and carried the casks over the equator twice, the flavor became suddenly palatable. As a teenager, I wasn't too concerned with the story of Linie Aquavit, but only appreciated how it helped me digest the bland dinner and gave me a buzz.

My dad viewed Norwegian dinner as a chance to extol the virtues of Scandinavian culture and give a history lesson about our relatives. He opened up great-grandfather Ellef's chest and pulled out stories of life in the New World.

"Here's my grandfather's 'Certificate of Citizenship,' when he became an American." My father then read the crumpled document, "I hereby renounce allegiance to the King of Sweden and Norway. Dated the 15th of July 1904." (This was the year before Norway's independence from the more powerful Sweden in 1905. We'd heard jokes about the rivalry between Norway and Sweden and that some Norwegians in the United States were furious at Sweden and called them "Swedish devils." My dad explained that "renouncing allegiance" was probably standard legal language for becoming a U.S. citizen.)

Even though he became American, Ellef might have lived a life in Minnesota essentially unchanged from Norway. He was surrounded by his countrymen, read Norwegian newspapers, and spoke his native language at home. His brother Johannes and sister Severina followed Ellef to the Midwest. My grandfather remembered that there were always new relatives from Scandinavia immigrating to Minnesota and sleeping on the floor of Ellef's house until they settled or moved on. In essence, Ellef was helping to colonize the vast stretches of midwestern land.

Ellef married a woman from Sweden whom he met at the Swedish Lending Library on Franklin Avenue. After talking over books, he took her dancing at the Norman Hall nearby and for a ride at the Wonderland Amusement Park at 31st Avenue and Lake Street. Minneapolis, this new city on the prairie, offered luxuries to Ellef that he never had back home in Norway. He could now re-create his image and impress his new Swedish girlfriend.

As we passed around the aquavit after dinner, we imagined Ellef and his Swedish girlfriend riding on a horse-drawn omnibus or simply strolling down the avenues by all the newly planted elms that would one day shade the streets of Minneapolis. Swedes and Norwegians can generally understand each other's languages, but maybe they spoke in English to impress each other with their skill.

My dad said they often teased his father about this "interracial marriage" because grandpa Al married a Swede as well. Even though he was already half Swedish himself, my grandfather considered himself Norwegian. He shrugged off the jabs of interracial marriage by saying, "In America, anything can happen."

Munch Is Dårlig

Our first visitors arrived right after we moved into our apartment. Wes, the man we knew from our Norwegian class in Cambridge, had been traveling by car with his friend Aud from Jessheim. Aud was a blonde middle-aged Norwegian woman with a barrel-chested laugh that filled the air. Wes and Aud couldn't stop at any more antique markets on the way home because the backseat of the car was packed with collectibles. The trunk was loaded with quilts that Aud had brought from home because she never liked the quilts that were provided at cabins along the route. They could only stay for the afternoon, as they had to get home. A grocery store in Jessheim was having a big sale on frozen salmon.

I asked Aud what she thought of our apartment with the sleek IKEA furniture that gave the rooms an airy feel. Aud apologized that she didn't like the barebones Scandinavian style with the uncomfortable furniture that was so popular. She then gave us a gift of some decorative table covers to liven up the place.

I held out hope that Aud would at least like the two classic Norwegian paintings by Edvard Munch, *The Madonna* and *The Kiss,* hanging on our living room wall. The swirling brush strokes around the enraptured figures embracing in *The Kiss* radiate the heated emotion of the moment, and the bare-chested, erotic *Madonna* shows a passionate Mary rather than the typically pious Blessed Virgin.

"Munch's paintings are *dårlig,*" Aud said straight-faced. "I'm not a good Norwegian, you see."

Dårlig? I asked Wes if that was like "darling," but he translated it as "ugly."

"But these two aren't so bad," Aud conceded. "I just like happier paintings."

I'd learned from my relatives in Minnesota that in Scandinavia we had to offer coffee to our guests right away. I brought out a pot of very strong coffee for Aud, Wes, and Katy. "I don't like it strong," Aud confessed. She gave out one of her hearty laughs after taking a sip. "In Norway, our coffee is much, much stronger."

I told Aud how my Swedish grandmother used to make coffee as weak as possible and often cracked an egg in the coffee to keep the grounds together and add flavor. Aud shook her head. "Eggs in coffee? Only in Sweden would they think of that."

Wes came bearing gifts. "Look, your relatives made marmalade," he said as he gave us an old tin canister. Emblazoned across the red cylinder in gold lettering was my last name, "DRÆGNI," so perhaps my distant relatives were jam and fruit juice magnates, and they surely needed an American representative for the company.

"They don't make Drægni marmalade anymore, though," Aud said, interrupting my daydream. "Perhaps because of their ad campaign: '*Alle spyr etter Drægni saft.*'" She explained that in the dialect of the Sognefjord, where the jam was made, this translated as "Everyone asks for Drægni juice." "But in regular *bokmål* Norwegian it means, 'Everyone vomits after Drægni juice.'" She laughed her hearty chuckle.

Wes opened our next gift, which was enclosed in a velvet pouch. He pulled out tiny glittering silver spoons that he and Aud had found at a *loppemarked* (flea market). He explained how the spoons had a very special Norwegian pattern and were quite valuable.

"These will be the perfect spoons for our coffee!" I said as I plopped in a spoonful of sugar and stirred. Wes and Aud stared at me as I realized that these were collectible spoons like my Swedish grandmother had displayed in her knickknack case.

Wes pulled out a pair of high-powered binoculars and asked if we wanted them in case we went hiking in the woods. Katy picked them up to have a look as Wes helped me take the empty coffee cups into the kitchen.

While piling the dirty cups on the counter, I told Wes that he should really hold on to the binoculars because Katy could be dangerous with them. "Our neighbors in the apartment complex across the alley are so close and they hardly ever shut their blinds," I said.

By the time we got back into the living room, Katy was hiding under the window and shutting the blinds. "Get down!" she said. "There's a little old lady out there who is furious at me for looking at her through binoculars."

I went out on the balcony and saw a woman shaking her fist at me. I waved, and she eventually walked away. Wes wisely took the binoculars back to Jessheim, and we didn't get booted out of Norway for breaking an unwritten law of *Janteloven*.

We weren't sure what to do with our new valuable silver spoons until we met Rachel and Arild. They had both attended the University of Minnesota but were now happy to be back in Trondheim and ready to settle down with their two-year-old son, William. "People in the U.S. were always trying to 'make something of themselves' and hurrying around to be successful," Rachel told us. "I've talked to people in Norway who are just happy to be in their position and don't really see the need to rush around so much."

Katy and I invited them over for coffee and to help us figure out the washing machine, which had text in Norwegian with obscure little drawings that were supposed to be universally understood. We showed Rachel the wash cycle we'd used, and she laughed. We'd been just rinsing our clothes for the past couple of weeks, not washing them. "You want to boil your clothes for about sixty minutes," she said, pointing to the *koke* button that means "boil" or "stew." Afterwards, our clothes were so clean that we washed them less for fear that they'd wear out.

Another mystery that Katy and I couldn't figure out was where to recycle our bottles. Every apartment building had bins for paper and cans, but none for bottles. "You threw them away?" Arild said. Almost all bottles are reused or recycled in Norway, and each could get us about 2.5 kroner, or about 40 cents, according to Arild. "A little town outside of Trondheim got an award as the best recycler in the country. Of course, they had garbage inspections, and people would be fined if they caught any bottles or cans in their trash." I was relieved that we hadn't been nabbed by the cops for flagrant recycling abuse.

Arild helped me brew up some coffee in the kitchen, and I told him that Norwegian coffee had a funny taste to it. He examined the bag of *Koffeinfri Kaffe* and pointed out that this was "caffeine-free" coffee. This explained why Katy and I had had splitting headaches the first week we were in Trondheim. It also showed the dire necessity to learn Norwegian.

We carried the steaming hot decaffeinated coffee into the living room and set it down with our new tiny silver spoons. Rachel lit up when she saw the spoons and told us that it was perfectly acceptable to use them. "The silver spoons are brought out only for very special guests either for coffee or *is* (ice cream). I give my goddaughter one silver spoon every year, and they are very expensive. I have it engraved, so she keeps a collection."

"When women get married they all have a collection of silver spoons as a sort of dowry," Arild said.

"I don't have any because I came from a poor village," Rachel added.

"Are you two married?" Katy asked.

Rachel explained that they are *samboer*, which means cohabitants, a living situation that is given automatic legal status in Norway. Nearly a half million Norwegians between ages twenty and thirty, about a fifth of the population, are *samboer*. Half of Norwegian kids are born out of wedlock. In 1951, only two thousand couples got divorced in the whole country. Fifty years later, more than half of all marriages in Norway end in divorce. In the past several years, statistics indicate that divorce has actually gone down, but it's not surprising because fewer people get married. This might explain why the Norwegian word *gift* can mean either "married" or "poison."

The acceptance of *samboer* probably began centuries ago in western Norway, where my great-grandfather Ellef grew up. Sons couldn't inherit the farm until after their parents died, so young couples often waited to formally wed until after their parents' deaths. If the bride wore a metal crown, it meant she didn't have a child yet. Otherwise, she wore a crown of ribbons that looked like a fool's cap to discourage other women from having children out of wedlock. Over the years, though, this became almost the standard wedding outfit for women. The Norwegian word *husbond* originally meant not only husband, but also the owner of the house and farm, while the word for wedded man is *ektemann*.

Even in Norway, the status of *samboer* wasn't recognized until recently. Until 1972, Norwegian law forbade a man and a woman to live together without being married. The couple could be thrown in jail and fined, although this "sleeping" law was rarely enforced. A new survey of Norwegian junior high and high school students by the *Adressavisen* newspaper found that one of their goals in life was to have children and be *samboer*—not married but *samboer*.

Rachel and Arild told us about new Norwegian terms: *partnerskap*, for "gay marriage," and *flerkulturelt ekteskap*, meaning "multicultural marriage." Arild's favorite term was *erdig pakke*, or "a ready package," which means a woman with at least one kid, so all the work of having kids is already done and the man can have an instant family.

Running the risk of looking like one of those couples who wants everyone else to get married, we asked Rachel if she wanted the silver spoons. We explained that we would probably just lose the spoons anyway. She was thrilled to have them, and Arild feigned interest. Somehow she "forgot" the spoons in our apartment, perhaps to be polite because she probably couldn't imagine anyone not wanting to keep their precious silver spoons.

Aliens

"I had always thought that Norway was completely organized and with-it," I told Rachel.

"What? It's exactly the opposite!" she responded. "You Americans are far more organized. When I came back to work in Norway, I didn't understand how the companies are able to actually function. So many things are disorganized, and everyone always wants to go on vacation or home early."

The bureaucrats at the "Population Control" office sent us to the "Alien Office" to fill out the necessary paperwork to stay in Norway for the year. By the time we arrived, however, the office was already closed. The summer hours were listed on the door: 10 a.m. to 2 p.m. and closed Tuesdays. With a long lunch break, the office was probably only open twelve hours a week. When we finally made it during their open hours, I asked the exasperated worker about how they managed to get such a great schedule.

"We complained because we have so much paperwork, so they gave us fewer hours to work. Now we are lucky, and the weather is so beautiful in the summer," he replied, looking at his watch in anticipation of closing time.

As in any immigration office, much of the paperwork seemed self-inflicted. To get a residency permit, we were required to submit the usual wallet-sized photos and photocopies of our passports. This time we were asked to produce our marriage license, which we didn't have with us.

"You don't have your marriage certificate? Why not?" the clerk asked suspiciously.

We didn't know that we needed to carry our marriage license with us to prove we were married.

"How else would we know?" he responded, a true bureaucrat.

We called Katy's friend Margaret in Minnesota, and she was able to dig through our files and find a copy to send certified mail.

The next snag at the Alien Office was our lack of a phone at our apartment. How could they contact us if we didn't have a phone number? But how could we get a phone if we didn't have residency?

First, we needed to call the telephone company from a pay phone next to one of the newspaper kiosks in the town center. There were no phone books, so Katy asked the man in the kiosk if she could borrow his. The gruff but efficient man shook his head and told us in perfect English that he didn't have a phone book and none of the pay phones had them. He told us that we needed to call the phone company to get a phone book, but he added, "You can't get a phone book unless you have a phone."

To escape this Kafkaesque bureaucracy, we visited our landlord, Arne, at his job at a downtown bank for some advice. Arne greeted us warmly and sympathized with our struggle to get settled. He loved a challenge, so he took out his cell phone and dialed with a vengeance.

Telenor, the phone company, confirmed what the man in the kiosk had told us: No phone? No phone book.

Arne cupped his cell phone as we told him that we just needed to get the phone hooked up. Arne returned to the polite but stern conversation with Telenor but made no headway. The telephone company wouldn't let Katy and me have a phone because we were foreigners without residency. His explanation that we couldn't get residency without a phone number was met with silence.

After numerous phone calls, Arne solved the problem. His son Trond agreed to put his name on the phone, so Telenor would have no problems with illegal foreigners. By the time we walked back to our apartment, the phone was already hooked up.

Arne had given me the number of Telenor, so I called up to get a phone book. Fortunately, the service representative spoke English. In a lilting Norwegian accent, she asked my name, but, of course, she couldn't find me in the system. I explained that the phone was under Trond's name, and she finally found the listing. She said she'd send a phone book out to Trond.

"No, no! *We* want the phone book!" I replied.

"I'm not sure I can do that since you're not in the system," she hesitated.

"Well, can you add me to the system?"

"But it's not your phone, is it?"

After discussing this impasse for fifteen minutes, she agreed to bend the rules by adding my name to the account so she could send us a phone book. "It won't be sent out until the end of September," she explained, "because the new phone books haven't been printed yet."

The phone book arrived in mid-October, and I claimed victory. Stuffed inside the book were overdue bills with late fees because Telenor had misspelled my name as "Eric Densel." When the phone rang and they asked for Mr. Densel, at least I knew it was a solicitor, and I could practice my fledgling Norwegian.

Katy and I thought we were over the bureaucratic hump, but then the Alien Office requested a copy of our bank statement to show that we had enough money to stay in Norway. We stopped downtown again to visit Arne at the bank.

We apologized for interrupting him at work again, but Arne replied, "At my age, you want to be interrupted." He served us some hair-raising coffee in small paper cups. Apparently, Norwegians don't use cream or sugar to cut the caffeine. After chatting for about half an hour, we told Arne that we'd like to open a bank account. He looked at his watch and said, "Now, it is three fifteen and banks are closed." Closed? "Yes, the bank is open until three o'clock in summer. We work seven and one half hours in winter, with one half hour for lunch. In summer, we work seven hours with a lunch break." He told us that we would have no problems opening an account the next day. We realized we were holding him overtime. "Oh, it's OK. You know in Norway, we work thirty-five hours a week. In the old days, I remember people worked forty hours a week, but it's too much. You have no life then. I want to see my family sometimes."

He told us that most Norwegians finish work no later than four o'clock so they can go hiking, skiing, sailing, or spend time with their kids. Most stores close by five — all the downtown bookstores are dark in spite of many people walking around. The only store that we found open on Sundays was a 7–Eleven, and there were no Sunday newspapers because the carriers didn't want to work on that day.

"Luckily, we have five weeks of vacation a year so we can enjoy life," Arne said. Retirement officially doesn't begin until sixty-seven years old, but anyone over sixty gets six weeks of vacation. "Some people call it the 'elderly vacation,'" he said. "We must — how do you say — have fun!"

Living the Norwegian Dream

A simple yearlong residency permit meant the Norwegian government would take care of us and pay for the birth of our first baby. A pamphlet we received from the Royal Ministry of Health and Social Affairs confirmed, "Compulsorily insured under the National Insurance Scheme are all persons resident or working in Norway."

No wonder Norway has had the highest quality of life rating for years. "It's not that we buy more things or have more things, it's that we are guaranteed a high standard of living," an American living in Oslo told me. "We don't have two cars, we take the bus; we can probably count the number of times that we go out to eat." While this may not be the American dream of wealth, Norway's system gives a degree of stability and certainty that your health care will be covered, free higher education will be provided, you won't be out on the street if you lose your job, and your pension will be paid by the government.

When Norway was declared to have the highest standard of living for three years in a row, the prime minister told the Norwegian people to stop complaining that they didn't have enough things. About the same time, the Norwegian government was considering a proposal to make public transportation — especially in Oslo — all free.

The welfare system was paid for by high taxes, especially income tax, which didn't seem to raise the rancor that it would in the United States. Many people in Norway were proud of their welfare system, but Norwegian modesty kept them from bragging. "It's the system we have chosen," Sissel, my second Norwegian teacher, told me matter-of-factly, "and I'm happy to pay the taxes for it."

Happy to pay taxes for welfare? I'd been surprised to hear nearly identical views from many Norwegians, which was one of the main reasons that Norway refused to join the European Union. No one wanted to give up this comprehensive welfare system that helped all Norwegians.

Growing up in Minnesota, I was always taught by my dad that Scandinavian society was some sort of utopian system that helps everyone. When asked why we were in Norway, I joked that Katy and I were on assignment to discover the secrets of the Norwegian welfare system by having a baby. Katy was not amused.

When my great-grandfather Ellef left the Lusterfjord, Norway was the poorest country in Europe. Norwegians left in droves; more than 750,000 emigrated. This was the largest per capita emigration from Europe after Ireland.

After the discovery of oil and natural gas in the 1960s, along with tapping into the country's waterways for hydroelectric power, Norway became the richest country in Europe. Thanks to the massive oil reserves found in the North Sea, Norway is the third largest oil exporter. "The rest of Europe calls Norwegians 'the blue-eyed Arabs,'" Knut told me. Rather than letting Phillips Petroleum do the drilling, the Norwegian government set up its own oil company, Statoil. The money goes into the *oljefondet* (oil fund) to support the government and keep taxes relatively low for this welfare system.

"Norway is rich not only because of Statoil," said Knut, "but also because as a country we've made a decision to share our resources with each other, like people in Sweden and Finland do. We're founded on a fusion between social solidarity and a democratic ideal. Therefore we don't have the poor like you do in the United States—or the crime, for that matter."

"Now in Norway we have oil and gas, so we are strong," our landlord, Arne, told me. "At least we think we are strong."

With the affluence came multinational corporations trying to capitalize on the newfound wealth. Arne was worried.

"Some of us Norwegians consider Norway to be the fifty-first state. Because we have McDonalds, Burger Kings, and all that, some Norwegians think that we're just like America."

I told him that I didn't see it that way. Norway has kept its character in spite of these growth spurts.

"That's good," he responded.

Still, I expected Norway to be clean and spotless like Switzerland. In general the farms and towns were tidy, but this new influx of fast food—O'Martins hamburger joints and 7–11 convenience stores—led to litter around these stores.

In a way, I was relieved to find a blemish on paradise, and thankful that Norway was relaxed and not too fastidious. In the balmy summer, hairy men fresh off the beach walked around the grocery without shirt or shoes. One day, I went into a Narvesen kiosk to buy a pen but couldn't find anyone to help me. I heard a toilet flush in back, and the clerk came out of the bathroom zipping up his fly and tucking in his shirt. When I offered to pay for one of the Bic pens, he let me keep it. "Shh, it is OK," he said.

In Norway, the concept of trespassing is vastly different. Swimmers can take a dip in the water no matter who owns the property, and hikers can supposedly camp out wherever they want for one night. I felt an air of permissiveness permeating the society that I thought made Norwegians far more relaxed than their American counterparts. That is, apart from the social norms of *Janteloven* to keep the people in line. Also, strict laws in some areas, such as those against alcohol, underscored the social engineering to try to better the country. Still, Norway has one of the lowest murder rates in the world, in spite of 720,000 registered firearms.

Those who do commit heinous crimes spend a maximum sentence of twenty-one years in prison. "But no one stays more than about five years in jail," my Norwegian teacher Sissel said only somewhat sarcastically. Rather than sometimes regressive punishments for the accused, the Norwegian government wants to reintegrate criminals into society so they aren't a burden. Therefore, criminals often spend five years in jail and get an education. "It's just like going to the university, only you leave jail without debt accrued from paying for room and board," Sissel said as she showed me a photo in our Norwegian textbook of a jail cell with homey wooden walls and a view of the fjord that looked better than student housing.

Being thrown in the clink in Norway isn't all bad, and the government picks up the bill. "See that?" a cab driver asked me one day pointing out the window. "That's Norway's second largest jail, but there are only about 10 percent Norwegians in there. The rest are people from other countries who come here and then commit a crime. It's really more like a hotel. They each have their own room with TVs and Internet access. Some have even studied to become lawyers while they were in jail, and the Norwegian government paid for everything. It's better to be a prisoner in a Norwegian jail than free in Albania or Belarus."

Despite some anti-immigrant feeling, newspapers reported that the population of Norway would actually decline without these new arrivals, and, once again, the welfare system accommodates them.

This social-democratic idea of wealth redistribution and equality extends to the workplace, where the wage gap between entry-level workers and CEOs doesn't begin to approach the obscene levels reached by many U.S. companies. Shannon, a Canadian living in Norway, said, "Back home when someone is rich and has been successful, people say, 'Good for you!' Here [in Norway], I feel that people are very jealous if someone makes a lot more money. Many don't even think that their boss should make more than they do. I think you lose the incentive here to get a higher education or take risks like starting your own business."

"Everyone's income is public knowledge and is even listed on the Internet," said Arild, an engineer for a small oil exploration business. I respond that people are probably very respectful of each other's privacy, right? "No way," he responded. "The day after they list income, everyone comes to work, and they are all very angry that so-and-so makes a little bit more. Often, it's not even a dollar more, but it causes many arguments."

Sissel added, "If you see that your neighbor [at work] makes a million kroner and the responsibilities in his job description don't really fit what he's being paid for, you can report them. This rarely happens, but the idea of it keeps people honest." *Janteloven* has found new legs with the Internet.

Does it keep salaries more even? "Yes," confirmed Arild, "but then people figure that a regular construction worker can go to work right away and get a paycheck because he requires no education. Compared to that of a higher-paid manager or engineer who gets years of education—and debt—the lifetime earning is about the same."

"I know a lot of people who live off the system and don't want to work," Rachel said. "They get a doctor to say that they're unable to work, and then they just receive money from the government."

I blushed because I was accepting the Norwegian government's health care and free university tuition. While I agreed with Sissel that I was "happy to pay taxes" because I was receiving so much in return, I soon understood what these higher taxes meant. Gasoline was five times what it cost in the U.S. The government even wanted to tax us on boxes of our own stuff that we shipped from Minnesota to ourselves in Norway. With this big government taxing—and helping—the Norwegians, it's no wonder that Oslo beat out Tokyo as the world's most expensive city.

Porridge Night

My grandfather Al used to dig his table knife into the stick of butter on the table and bring a big dollop to his lips. Butter is the ultimate candy to a Norwegian. Sandwiches are even called *smørbrød:* butter bread.

According to old records from the Lusterfjord, where my great-grandfather Ellef lived, tenant farmers would have to work off their *smør skatt,* or butter tax, depending on how much butter they'd used. Butter was currency, and people's addiction to this sweet cream luxury held them in debt.

In the Norwegian cookbook that Katy and I bought, almost half of the recipes were for butter-filled pastries and cakes. The number of vegetable recipes was scanty, and main course recipes were mostly meat. The first chapter of the book was packed with recipes for different kinds of porridge of rice and other grains. The text of the cookbook joked that if you eat too much porridge over your lifetime, you will begin to look like it. We had no need to worry about that; Katy didn't want any gruel served in our apartment. I then understood at least part of the saying "Danes live to eat; the Norwegians eat to live; and the Swedes eat to drink."

I showed the cookbook to Arild and Rachel, expecting them to be revolted, but they drooled over the variety of porridge recipes: oat porridge, buttermilk porridge, barley flour porridge, velvet porridge, caramelized porridge, semolina porridge, rice porridge, and sour cream porridge.

"Oh, that last one is the best: *rømmegrøt!*" Rachel exclaimed.

"But don't Norwegians usually eat slices of bread with cheese for breakfast?" I asked.

"Porridge is for dinner! It's the main course," she replied. "We eat it without salad, bread, or anything else. Just porridge. *Rømmegrøt.* Sometime we'll have you over for porridge!"

Katy looked at me desperately and subtly shook her head.

"We tried to make *rømmegrøt* in the States," Rachel continued, "but we couldn't find sour cream with enough fat in it. You need at least 30 percent fat, and all the sour cream there is just 7 percent."

I could see that Katy, being pregnant, was especially nauseated. I told Rachel that my dad fed us *rømmegrøt* once for Norwegian dinner, but no one liked it.

Rachel was disappointed. She paused for a minute and said, "Obviously, you haven't had good *rømmegrøt*. We will make you the good porridge. Saturday night! We'll see you around five, then."

After Rachel and Arild left, Katy asked, "How on earth did we just get talked into going to eat gruel?"

Katy and I braced ourselves for the bizarre fatty flavors of a true Norwegian dinner at Rachel and Arild's. I bought some of the traditional cheeses, so we could prepare our palates ahead of time. We relished the golden delicious Jarlsberg cheese, which is like a creamy Swiss cheese without the bite. The *Gudbrandsdalsost* cheese, sometimes called *gjetost* (goat cheese) or simply *brunost* (brown cheese), made our mouths pucker with super sweet and rich caramel flavor.

We put our hopes on the *gammelost*, or old cheese, made from sour milk, in hopes that it'd be like a scrumptious Camembert or Gorgonzola. The aroma that wafted into my nostrils from the round, brown splotchy cheese was not unlike sweaty tennis shoes. I smeared some on a cracker and plopped it in my mouth. Katy watched as I chewed the stinky mess. I was her guinea pig before she dared eat it. "What's it taste like?" she asked.

"Like a grainy sweat sock soaked in cream," I responded. I then understood why *gammelost* is rarely sold in the U.S.

When we arrived at Rachel and Arild's house, their two-year-old son was jumping from pillow to pillow on the couch. "Saturday night is 'candy night,'" Rachel said. William could eat as much candy as he wanted, but only on Saturday night. Rachel explained that this was a Saturday Norwegian tradition—to fill up a bag from the candy display at the grocery store and then watch evening cartoons while eating porridge. William started with cake, his favorite, and then moved on to a caramel sucker, a Kinder chocolate egg, and a lollipop that was dipped in pop rocks. His actions speeded up with each bite, but Rachel reassured me, "He'll sleep fine after this."

Most of the candy was not so different from what we could find in the U.S., except for the licorice. I love strong, dark licorice, but I had to spit it out into my napkin because I thought something was wrong with it. A salty flavor lingered and almost stung my tongue. Arild laughed, "Once you learn to love salt licorice, then you're truly Norwegian."

To wash down the bitter, salty taste, I opened a bottle from the six-pack of beer that we had brought. The beer was named Munkholmen (Monk Island), so I figured it would be like the strong Belgian ales brewed by monks.

"It's actually very good nonalcoholic beer," Arild told me.

"What? It's nonalcoholic?" I said, and Arild pointed out the word *alkoholfritt øl* on the label.

"Many people drink this when they go out because you can't drink and drive here," Rachel said.

Katy pointed out that you shouldn't drink and drive in the U.S. either. Arild said that you can't drink *anything* before driving in Norway or it'll put you over the legal limit. "They say that if you take a chocolate with alcohol in it, or a cake with liquor inside, it's too much."

"You can't even drink and ride your bikes in Norway," Rachel added. "There are very stiff penalties."

I'd seen the "beer curtain" at the little Rimi grocery store near our apartment. After 8 p.m., the metal grate is pulled down so customers can only pine for the bottles behind it. I thought that Norway had become less restrictive, though, because the Vinmonopolet liquor store no longer kept all the liquor behind a wall, so now shoppers could examine the bottles before purchasing.

As the legend goes, strong aquavit was introduced to Norway by the archbishop himself. The thoughtful Danish leader Eske Bille was occupying Bergenhus Castle in 1531 and sent a bottle of "Aqua Vitae" to the archbishop as a sort of medicine. Apothecaries in Norway began to sell the alcohol with infusions of herbs to help various ailments, and patients soon lined up to get their medicine. Industrious Norwegians began distilling their own aquavit, and by 1827 approximately eleven thousand stills were pumping out homemade liquor. Drunkenness became a grave social problem, according to many newspapers of the time, so homemade alcohol was outlawed in 1845, and most of the distilleries were destroyed.

Historically speaking, I'd heard that many immigrants — perhaps even my great-grandfather Ellef — were relieved to be out of Norway because of the excessive drinking. The Norwegian temperance movement went further when teetotalers were able to outlaw both whisky and fortified wine from 1916 until 1927. After that, all wine and liquor had to be sold through the public "Vinmonopolet," which were only in the larger towns. Customers could browse through a white catalog printed on newspaper and then order through a little window inside the store.

The state-owned Vinmonopolet in Trondheim has marble counters to display the alcohol and wine. A bottle of Norwegian Linie Aquavit costs U.S. $19.95 at East Lake Liquor in south Minneapolis, but the same bottle costs more than $40 at the Vinmonopolet in Trondheim. This huge chunk of tax helps fund anti-drinking advertisements and treatment clinics for alcoholics, and sometimes, as in Kristiansand, the detox center is right next to the Vinmonopolet.

Even so, I'd seen antsy junior high girls waiting outside the Vinmonopolet for a haggard drunkard to stumble out of the store with a bottle of Absolut Vodka for them. They jumped up and down excitedly when they got their prize, and the man got to keep another bottle as payment. This scene could have been replayed anywhere in the U.S., because the Norwegian drinking age is eighteen for beer and wine and twenty for liquor.

Arild told us that the town he comes from is right next to Sweden, but custom agents rarely guard the border. "When some friends got married, they went into Sweden to buy cases of alcohol and then drove an hour out of their way through my town to avoid the customs."

I asked Arild if Norwegians still make home-brewed aquavit. "No, no one does that," Arild responded. "They all make— how is it in English?— 'moonshine.' You know, they mix yeast, sugar, and water so it is like 180 proof. Many people where I come from make it in their garage."

Rachel interrupted, "But they don't drink that in the cities, like Trondheim."

Arild said, "Oh, yes, they do! People come to parties with one bottle of, say, Coca-Cola and a clear plastic bottle of homemade." He pointed to a one-and-a-half liter bottle of Solo orange pop. "You think about it, if this were full of moonshine, you could get ten people drunk for two nights. How much would that cost with alcohol from the store?"

"But do the police catch them?" Katy asked.

"Oh, they try," Arild said.

"Didn't they catch some people recently in Trondheim?" asked Rachel.

"That was different," responded Arild. "That was for fake liquor from Poland and the Czech Republic that they would put into Absolut Vodka bottles, reseal the top, then sell it illegally in Norway. People were dying from it or going blind because there was some methyl alcohol inside. The police asked anyone who had bought these bottles to please come to the station and they wouldn't press charges. People drank the liquor anyway and kept dying!"

I took another sip of my Munkholmen beer and now didn't mind that it was alcohol-free.

The *rømmegrøt* was finally ready. Rachel brought out a big steaming pot, and we all sat around the coffee table and watched a Saturday evening cartoon. By this time, little William wasn't hungry anymore and was indeed sleepy. Rachel served up a bowl for each of us, sprinkled cinnamon on top, and added a big pat of butter onto the rich cream porridge. To cut the rich flavor, we ate salty pieces of salami and drank sugary orange soda pop (without moonshine). Fortunately, Arild and Rachel didn't serve any sweet brown goats milk cheese or the smelly *gammelost* to overpower our taste buds; the *rømmegrøt* did that, with the power of butter. I could feel my heart slowing down with each cholesterol-filled bite of this Norwegian comfort food that tasted like buttery bread dough that refused to be cut by my teeth. I worried that if I told Rachel that the *rømmegrøt* was fantastic, she might invite me back for another porridge night. Instead, I had learned to just be silent.

Norsk Course

Floor-to-ceiling panes of glass in the classrooms gave sweeping views of pine forests and the frigid water in the Trondheim-fjord. The thought of all-day language classes in the height of summer pained us when we remembered the Norwegian advice to take advantage of every ray of sun before the *mørketid,* or dark time of winter.

A towering blonde woman with rigid posture carried a stack of books confidently into the classroom. She set her books on the teacher's desk and pronounced, "*Hei, god dag. Jeg heter Solveig.*" She then went into a long spiel in Norwegian that only the Germans seemed to comprehend. Katy and I stared at her blankly and considered bolting for the door to avoid the monthlong torture to make us talk.

Michael, a German student with a scraggly beard, fraying jeans, and Birkenstock sandals, asked her in English, "Excuse me, does your name 'Solveig' mean 'silver' in Norwegian?"

Solveig realized that we were a beginning class and apologized in English, the common language of everyone there. "No, my name is terrible. It means 'the one who keeps the keys.'"

Michael assured her, "Oh, I think it's a very pretty name. Solveig. I like it." I couldn't believe that Michael was trying to pick up our teacher within the first five minutes of class.

Juri, an Italian rugby player from Genoa, interrupted, "Excuse me, excuse me. I have a very important question to ask. How many bottles of wine can my friend bring when he comes to visit from Italy?"

Solveig struggled, "Umm . . . two. Maybe three . . . I'm not sure."

"In the U.S., it's two," I added.

Two students from Prague argued loudly in Czech with phlegm-filled guttural sounds as if they were threatening each other by clearing their throats. Solveig asked one of them, Marianne, what the problem was. Because a Czech-Norwegian dictionary didn't exist, Marianne had to look up the word first in her Czech-German dictionary and then her German-Norwegian dictionary. She wrote her question on the board, and we looked in our English-Norwegian dictionary to translate. "Does Jägermeister liquor count as one of the bottles?"

A big discussion ensued about what liquor students had brought in and how the prices in Norway were double anywhere else. Yvonne from Stuttgart wondered, "Everyone at the discotheque last night was drunk. How can they get drunk if it costs so much?"

"I think that if they drink, they drink a lot," Michael said.

"And you don't in Germany?" teased Johann from France.

All the students blurted out their opinion of the other nations' drinking habits as Solveig watched silently. She didn't raise her voice but stayed still to regain control. "In Norwegian, this is what we call, 'helt Texas,' meaning 'whole Texas' or total chaos."

The class laughed. She said that the restrictions about importing liquor are "all politics." Juri didn't know this last word, so I translated it into Italian *politica,* but he didn't understand what politics had to do with Jägermeister.

"Politics!" Solveig exclaimed, exasperated. "You know, like your old prime minister in Italy: Berlusconi."

Juri stood up, indignant. "What! Berlusconi? Excuse me *professoressa,* but I did not travel halfway around the world to be insulted! He is not my prime minister. I did not vote for him nor did anyone I know." He gathered up his textbooks to protest the turn of the discussion.

The Germans calmed him down, saying, "Imagine if your president was Bush!" Katy and I squirmed in our seats.

Solveig saved us, "Yes, it's *helt Texas* in America now."

The Germans laughed, but Juri kept his arms crossed because he was still upset that Solveig had mentioned Berlusconi. Solveig restored calm to the classroom by staring quietly at all of us. "Now we shall learn adjectives," she proclaimed, and used metaphors such as "clever as a fox" or "quick as a rabbit." When she got to the expression *Sta som et esel,* meaning "stubborn as a mule," the European students opened their dictionaries to search for the word *mule.*

"You mean *donkey,*" Johann said.

Solveig explained that it was a donkey that was the cross between a horse and a mule.

"No, no, no, no," Juri said. "Mule is the mixture." Solveig looked to Katy and me for the correct word in English, and I confessed that I hadn't given it much thought.

"My dictionary says, *jackass* or *ass,*" Yvonne pointed out.

"How do you say that in French?" Johann wondered aloud.

"Well, what is a burro then?" Michael asked.

"Burro? That's butter? What has butter to do with ass?" Juri retorted as he gestured wildly.

As the multilingual discussion raged, Solveig sat down in her chair and looked at her watch.

A to Å

The more Norwegian words I memorized, the more confused I became. Our second lesson was how to tell time in Norwegian, but I soon learned that they counted backwards from the hour rather than added on to it. For example, when I asked what time the bus came at the information booth in downtown Trondheim, the answer was *"Ti på halv to,"* meaning ten to halfway to two. That was 1:30 minus ten minutes, which was 1:20. On top of that, they officially use the twenty-four-hour clock, so that could only mean 1:20 in the morning. By the time I figured out what time it was, the bus had already gone and we were late for class.

I tried to show off my Norwegian by saying we arrived on the late bus, but rather than saying *sent* (late), I said *sint* (angry).

"Excuse me? Why is the bus so angry?" Solveig asked.

The most difficult part of Norwegian for me was pronouncing the vowels correctly. A simple slipup and I referred to someone not as *du* (you) but as a toilet *(do)*.

To add to the confusion, Norwegian has three extra vowels at the end of the alphabet: ø, æ, and å. From A to Z in Norwegian becomes from A to Å. One-syllable expressions vary radically, or so I was told, with a slight change of vowel sound. *Uff Da!* was very different from *Huff Dah!* as was *Ah!* from *Åh!* (pronounced "Oh!").

I learned that the word for "Wow!" is *Oy!* (pronounced Oh-ay-ee), so I threw it into any conversation I could. When a Norwegian classmate told me that her grandmother had been sick, I said, *"Oy!"* and shook my head in sympathy. She looked at me strangely and said that *Oy!* should only be used for good news.

While "yes" was simply *ja* in Norwegian, the sound was made by breathing in, not out, like most words. *Ja* sounded like a sigh and a relaxing, deep breath. Katy and I wanted to sound like true Norwegians, so we practiced breathing in *Ja*. I gasped and felt like I swallowed a bug. As I was choking, Solveig offered me some water and asked if I was OK.

Solveig told us that this intensive five-week course usually took an entire semester, so we had to put in more class time than expected. To avoid having class on Saturday and Sunday, she suggested that we just skip lunch and breaks every day. Katy and I agreed with the Germans that this sounded like a good idea. The Italians and the French thought this was a joke. Juri spoke up, outraged. *"Porca miseria, no!* I am very used to eating. I need to eat my lunch. I am not like you people who eat a sandwich on your feet like a horse. No, no, no."

In the end, Juri won out. We planned to have our last two lessons over the weekend. Even so, he showed up late to class on the last Sunday. He told us that he was at the disco until 4 a.m. with Johann. Both Juri and Johann were surprised by the strong women who stood up to men. "You people have very strange customs here in Norway! In Italy, we think that blonde Scandinavian women are goddesses, but I learned this is not true! Norwegian women are very dangerous." Juri held up his index finger to warn us. "At the disco, I saw a woman hit a man — poff! — right in the face. I think he was probably drunk, but still . . . I know that I'm going to be very careful around Norwegian women now."

Michael the German said that he would have hit her back. Juri put up his hand to stop him. "But no! You cannot hit a woman."

Solveig said that it was probably just a strange situation, but Juri interrupted. "I know it is probably not always this way in the discotheque, but I have been one time, so it is 100 percent for me that Norwegian woman hit the man."

For this last day of class, we all pushed our desks to form a long table to eat together. Solveig put on a CD of her favorite

Norwegian band, and we all read the words to the song "Eat Me Raw," which was supposedly about food. The graphic lyrics equated munching on vegetables with nibbling on genitalia. "I think there's a double meaning here, but isn't it just fun?" Solveig said.

We'd all chipped in to buy flowers for Solveig, and Yvonne had the big bouquet of daisies hidden under her desk. "Who's going to give it to her?" she whispered. Michael volunteered, but everyone wanted Juri to do it.

After dozing off a bit after lunch, Juri took the flowers and gave an eloquent speech about how much she had taught us and how we'd now be prepared for life in Trondheim. She beamed and said, "This will go lovely in my new house out in the country with a grass roof." As she accepted the flowers, she gave Juri a kiss on both cheeks. The class oohed and aahed. "You see," she said, "not all Norwegian women hit men."

The final test of the course lasted six hours. Katy had flat-out refused to take it. "Honestly. Why on earth would I want to take a six-hour test, when I'm painfully pregnant, to get a piece of paper that means nothing to me?"

We were lucky, because other university finals in Norway can last up to eight hours straight. No breaks are allowed, but students can eat sandwiches under the watchful eyes of Solveig and the other instructors. Teachers even followed students to the toilets and waited outside the stall listening attentively in case students had a book stashed behind the toilet. My vision blurred, and my writing hand cramped after the marathon exam. At the end of the six hours, we handed in our blue books full of Norwegian scribbling. Juri, Serena, Michael, and the other students all looked dazed but relieved that the exam was over. Solveig told us, "Now, you go out in Trondheim and speak Norwegian!"

We had studied *bokmål*, which is standard "book language" Norwegian and more Danish in flavor, due to the lengthy occupation by the Danes. *Bokmål* is spoken by about 90 percent of Norwegians and the prevailing language used in newspapers and books. However, language purists prefer *Nynorsk*, which combines the many dialects into an older, arguably more authentic Norwegian language. I simply wanted to communicate.

Wolfgang, the German organizer for the international students, just chuckled. "Once you finally learn your nice *bokmål* Norwegian, you will be so proud that you can start your university classes," Wolfgang said. "Then at your first lesson, you will have an instructor who speaks *Nynorsk*, and you won't understand a thing. Your next lesson will be taught by a Dane, and the other Norwegians will understand, but you won't. Then a Swedish professor will teach your next class, and you won't understand because he's, well, Swedish. Finally, you'll get a teacher who speaks *bokmål* like you learned in class, but the professor speaks in the dialect of Trondheim, and even the other Norwegians will have a hard time understanding. In any case, you'll survive."

I refused to believe that learning Norwegian was quite so futile as Wolfgang professed. Wasn't he supposed to be giving us a pep talk? Another Norwegian teacher, Sissel, confessed that Wolfgang was somewhat correct because *bokmål* is more of a big-city Oslo language. Sissel said, "If someone talks *bokmål* out on the street, everyone thinks, 'Who are you trying to impress? Talk dialect!'" She said that teachers have to make a conscious decision to speak *bokmål* and then change right back when the other teachers are around.

I assumed the local dialect, *Trøndersk*, was essentially a thick accent, but I learned that it is one of the most difficult out of the three hundred dialects in Norway. A flyer near our apartment advertised dialect lessons just for our neighborhood of Lademoen, Møllenberg, and Bakklandet. Astrid, a friend who lived in Møllenberg, explained how many consonants are dropped in Trondheim. For example, to say, "I'm in class too," which is "*Jer er i klassen, jeg også*" in standard Norwegian, is "Æ E I A Æ Å" in *Trøndersk*. I waited for her to explain that this was a joke, but she nodded earnestly.

I kept trying to decipher the language and thought I could learn Norwegian through comic books. Our friend Arild brought over a couple of Mickey Mouse and Donald Duck comics. "I have many more if you need to borrow them," he said.

Rachel added, "You don't need to give them back either," but Arild only scowled. I could relate to Arild's love for his comics, so I returned them in a week and didn't ask for more.

I still needed a regular Norwegian conversation partner and couldn't afford to hire a language teacher. When I came across brochures at the university that said "*Hjelp!* (Help!) No one to speak with? Feel alone?" I considered meeting with a depression therapist just to improve my conversational skills. I was spared from a prescription of Zoloft when solicitors began calling our recently listed phone number and I could babble with them for a half hour while they were being paid. I began dialing up toll-free numbers just to practice my phone proficiency.

On the other hand, Katy wasn't too concerned with perfecting the language and didn't spend hours memorizing verb charts like I did. She just learned a few key expressions: *Hyggelig å hilse på deg!* (Nice to meet you) and *Kjempebra!* (Fantastic!). She used the first line when she met someone, and the second in a pause in the conversation. Inevitably, she'd be praised with, "*Oi!* You speak Norwegian so well!"

In the pharmacy, I asked for some moisturizing lotion, and the clerk asked if I wanted facial cream. I had practiced the correct word to respond, "*hånd*," and rubbed my hands together to show how I'd use the lotion. I mispronounced the "å" and replied, "No, I'll use it on my *hund*."

"What? You're going to smear lotion all over your dog?" she said in English. "Why would you do that? Who puts lotion on their *hund*?"

Other customers stared at me, disturbed, as I put up my hands to show what I meant and repeated, "*Hund! Hund!*"

"*Hånd,*" the clerk said, finally understanding. Then she said something that was often repeated to me: "Please, please. Speak English. It's easier that way."

Cabin Culture

Our landlord and banker, Arne, theorized that the reason we had trouble relating to Norwegians in the city of Trondheim was that everyone would rather be in the countryside. "When we go walking up in the hills, we say 'hello' to everyone, and they say 'hello' to us. We're all very happy there." Then he laughed. "When I see those same people down in the city, I don't know them."

Arne spoke as if the stifling *Janteloven* only applied when in the city, but everyone was freed from these social constraints in the countryside. We followed Arne's advice to go to the enormous Bymarka park above town to see if Norwegians are truly friendlier and happier in the woods. The rickety old tram left downtown Trondheim and huffed and puffed its way up into the hills. The other trolley tracks in town had been dismantled, but hiking aficionados and streetcar lovers managed to preserve the last line, up to the national park.

A group of elderly women adorned with hand-knit sweaters struggled to get on the streetcar at the next stop; one of them even had a walker with wheels. They were each armed with two ski pole–like walking sticks for trekking through the forest.

We carried an enormous rucksack on the advice of our friend Henning. "Before going anywhere, you need to carry the 'Norwegian backpack,'" he had advised us. "Inside you have an umbrella or raincoat, a sweater, a swimsuit, and a *smørbrød* [sandwich]. Then you are ready for anything!" Optional accessories are a thermos filled with coffee (no cream!) and a little Norwegian flag.

At each stop closer to the nature reserve, the passengers seemed more animated and friendly. After twenty minutes, the *trikk*, or tram, came to the end of the line, and everyone hurriedly stepped off the streetcar and began stretching. "*God tur!*" (Have a good walk!) exclaimed the ladies as they cheerily marched out into the dense forest. I heard them chatter away, almost as if they wanted to break into song under the canopy of pines. They planted their canes into the grass with each step and scurried up the hill. Soon, they were out of sight, as they hiked much faster than we could, even though one of them got around with her walker.

Unmarked paths wandered through the woods, where Norwegians were busy picking blueberries or wild strawberries. Seemingly immune to the frigid cold water, teenagers leaped happily into the lakes, called *innsjøer*, or "inland seas." Beyond the trolley station, no restrooms disturbed the natural surroundings. Being pregnant, however, Katy wasn't thrilled to squat outside, so we planned our route to stop frequently at a wooden lodge for hot chocolate and waffles with strawberries and *rømme*.

Our landlord, Arne, was right. Hikers greeted us happily in the woods. The dark, stylish clothes of the city had been shed for brightly colored sweaters and hiking boots. One couple even stopped for a chat and told us, "Some trekkers like more remote places. There's a famous quote in Norwegian that 'I went on a hike but it was ruined when I saw another person.' Now, if you want a real Norwegian experience, you need to spend time in a *hytte*, or cabin."

After trekking in the Bymarka park amid outgoing Norwegians, we took the streetcar back into Trondheim for a swim at the Pirbadet pool. The giant windows of the pool overlooked the fjord, and whirlpools of fresh- and saltwater from the fjord relaxed our muscles after the walk in the park. We weren't the only ones who had come to relax; I recognized two hefty men from our hike who were now perched on the highest—and hottest—bench of the cedar-covered sauna. My eyes ached and skin itched from the 190 degree Fahrenheit heat, but the big men stoically resisted as they discussed their cabins near the remote mining town of Røros.

"Oh, I'm so sore from hiking to our *hytte*," said the man who had several rolls of stomach overlapping the top of his swimming trunks. "It's one kilometer from the nearest road."

"Only one? Ours is three kilometers away from where we park, all uphill," responded the other, sitting up straight to show off his barrel chest.

"Well, we only have three rooms in our cabin, so we all sleep next to the fireplace." Sweat flowed over his belly like little waterfalls.

"Our *hytte* just has one big room," replied his friend. He whisked away the beads of perspiration on his brow, perhaps annoyed that his body was giving in to the heat.

"Really? My wife wants to put electricity in our *hytte*, but I ask, what's the point of being in nature then?"

"*Nei*, you don't want electricity! We don't have it—or plumbing either."

"We do have moose, though. They eat our garden every year."

"Moose? You should be eating them!"

The temperature in the sauna had risen to 215. As I stood up, the blood rushed from my head, and little glints of light flitted in front of my eyes. When I dizzily pushed the door open, these two men were still boasting about the primitiveness of their respective *hytte*. They didn't dare be the first to admit that the sauna was too hot for them.

In the next few weeks, we heard more and more about how we needed to go to a *hytte* for the true Norwegian experience. Knut and Inger talked about their family *hytte*, where they spend four to five weeks in the summer. The *hytte* shouldn't be a massive lake home with all the amenities but must be spartan and isolated. The more remote, the better. *Hytte* culture involves wearing *hyttaklær*, ragged old "cabin clothes." Inger teased Knut, "Your *hyttaklær* at the cabin are mostly just your old clothes from the eighties. It's like a bad retro music video filmed in the fjords."

Øyvind, a high school teacher we met, glowed when discussing his cabin. "We have a great *hytte* that's three hours' walk from the closest road," he told me. His *hytte* is right near the park where *National Geographic* wanted to take pictures of musk oxen. The photographer couldn't carry all his equipment, however, and Norwegian law prohibits motors in the park. No cars, snowmobiles, helicopters, or ATVs are allowed. The magazine wasn't going to do an article, but then they found a loophole in the law: in the case of national interest, they could go in with a tank. Øyvind shook his head at the thought of American journalists insisting on being carried into the park and told us the *National Geographic* article had been put on hold. "I don't understand why you Americans want to always be so pampered," he said. "Our *hytte* has no running water, no electricity. We wouldn't want that. For water, we just drink from the stream; it's the best water there is!"

Michael from our Norwegian language course had a similar story about the water when he went exploring with Norwegian students at a *hytte* near Røros. "We had a great weekend! We had to walk for a few kilometers through a swamp, so our feet were soaking wet, but we learned how to put a grass roof on a *hytte*! We drank the water in the little pond there. It looked kind of yellow, but the Norwegians said that all the water in the wilderness should be OK to drink." He paused with a worried look on his face and put his hand on his stomach. "Well, I haven't gotten sick yet."

While most Norwegians are unfazed by a little dirt in the water, many squeamish foreigners aren't. Charlie, a professor from Milwaukee, described the *hytte* he visited perched on a cliff and how he climbed down a ladder to fetch water. After breaking the thin layer of ice, he lowered a bucket into the lake and pulled it back up with a rope. Tadpoles swimming in circles were scooped out. "The water was pretty funky tasting. We didn't drink it. I think that people assume the water is fine unless someone gets sick, then they test it."

In spite of these warnings, I planned a trip to a nearby *hytte* that was available to students. Being pregnant, Katy was skeptical. "Remember, we can't go too far into the woods, because I'm sure you don't want to have to carry me out three hours while I'm in labor."

Just when we were planning our trip, another classmate, Johann, told me about his trip. "Oh, it was terrible!" he said. "Elisabetta and I wanted to go to one of the student *hytte*. We got a late start and left at about four o'clock in the afternoon. Elisabetta asked me if I was sure I could find it, and I said that they had shown me where it was. Anyway, I had a compass and a map, so I thought I could. The paths were all wet and muddy and overgrown. It started getting dark at about seven, and we were completely lost. We turned back toward the car. For two hours, we wandered around in the dark until we found the car."

With these stories in mind, Katy and I delayed indefinitely our trip to a remote *hytte* until our baby could walk on his own. Instead, we took the tram again up to the hills for another hike. Everyone greeted us, and we even saw Johann and Elisabetta happily walking around the lake.

A True Norwegian

At the university in Trondheim, I signed up for a class on immigration and the offspring of immigrants. Especially, emigration from Norway to America. Specifically to Minnesota. In other words, they were studying me.

I explained that I had come to Norway to study them and how Norway had changed. My Norwegian classmates just smiled and took notes. I was under scrutiny along with my forefathers who left Scandinavia.

One student, Astrid, was writing her thesis on the Norwegian immigrants in Spring Grove, Minnesota, the town where my parents lived when I was born. She wanted to know all about this tiny town that was fiercely proud of its status as the first Norwegian settlement in the state. I only knew they had a scary Viking statue with different colored eyes and another statue of a drunk with a giant paunch emblazoned with the words "Belly by Budweiser."

We watched the movie *Fargo* to learn about the Minnesotan accent and how the reserved characters seemed to move in slow motion. The Norwegian students couldn't hear the difference in the pronunciation, perhaps because theirs was so similar.

"I have relatives in Minnesota," one student told me. "Bobby? Robby? Robert? Something like that. Why is everyone in the U.S. named 'Bob'?"

My new classmates were disappointed I wasn't the "typical American," who, apparently, was overweight, loud, and packed heat. I wasn't much help, because I couldn't justify U.S. foreign policy, I didn't own an American flag, but I did reinforce one stereotype as I stumbled through the Norwegian language.

I told my fellow classmates that Katy and I were even mistaken for foreigners when we walked down the streets of Marquette, Iowa. "Where are you folks from?" an Iowan had asked us. "Oh, I thought you must be Swedish or Norwegian because you're so thin and hardly anybody walks here."

The professor of the Norwegian immigration class hailed from Ohio. Professor Mauk had traveled to Minnesota to study Norwegian Americans, who, apparently, loved to be studied. For a valid historical survey, Professor Mauk had a hard time finding Norwegian Americans who were indifferent about their ancestry and weren't members of Sons of Norway. "When I finally did find some," he told the class, "they kept saying, 'Why do you want to talk to me? You should talk to someone who's actually interested in being Norwegian.' The more I'd talk to them, though, the more they realized what a difference their ancestry had made for them."

He told us that Norwegian Americans had the largest percentage of settlers in rural areas, probably because most Norwegians live outside of the cities even though only 3 percent of the land in Norway is arable. "Most of them came from the countryside before going to America. For example, do any of you come from cities in Norway?" he asked the class, and about half of the students raised their hands. "Hmm, let's say a city is at least as large as Tromsø with sixty thousand people."

Only two students kept their hands in the air. "Oh no, that's so big!" said Sophie, a spunky student from Nordfjord with blonde curly hair. "My city only has six thousand people."

Professor Mauk pointed out that some of the traditional Norwegian communities in the Midwest—like Spring Grove; Decorah, Iowa; and Westby, Wisconsin—have held on to Norwegian culture from a hundred years ago, and Norwegian historians go to these communities to learn dialects that no longer exist in Norway.

When I referred to the Norwegian Americans in these towns, Professor Mauk politely corrected me. "When I was in

Minnesota, no one ever called themselves that. They always referred to themselves simply as 'Norwegians.' Imagine if you told your fellow students here that you are 'Norwegian.'"

I told Helen, another university student, how people in Minnesota considered themselves Norwegian even if they'd never been to Norway or didn't speak a word of the language. Without a hint of irony, she responded. "Then you are Norwegian now." I argued that I'm American with Norwegian roots, but she didn't agree. "You were Norwegian first," she said.

"What does it mean to be American?" Professor Mauk interjected. "What to you is truly good about America?"

I was stumped. I mentioned the clichés of "freedom," "melting pot," "representative government."

"What about your Constitution?" Astrid asked.

"The Freedom of Information Act!" exclaimed Dag, an outspoken intellectual with his hair combed forward. "That is what makes America great."

I realized that Professor Mauk was leading us to one of the big questions of the day in Norwegian newspapers: What did it mean to be "Norwegian" when new immigrants to Norway refused to give up the culture of their native country. As in the U.S., some people viewed this as a threat to national unity, while others viewed this as building an exciting diverse society of immigrants.

In fact, the Norwegian word for foreigners is *innvandrere*, which sounds like "invaders." Sophie pointed out that "it's *vandre*. That's more like wander, so it's people who wander in." Sophie assured me that I wasn't a foreigner and that I was Norwegian because my great-grandfather was born here. I gave up arguing against this claim and realized this meant that I was accepted, even though other immigrants seemed to be necessarily excluded.

While Sophie was sure about my "Norwegianness," she wasn't sure about Professor Mauk. He spoke Norwegian fluently, lived in Norway, was even married to a Norwegian, but wasn't Norwegian. "I thought that the only people who really cared about Norway were those with Norwegian heritage," she said to the class.

Professor Mauk answered, "People keep asking me if I have become a Norwegian citizen yet, so I thought up a pat answer, 'Would you consider me more Norwegian then?' They pause to wonder if it's a trick question and then reply, 'Probably not.' Then they stop asking if I've become Norwegian."

Paul Bunyan's Blacksmith?

The Anglo-American settlers, who were already established in Minnesota, considered the new Norwegian immigrants to be smelly brutes and often not even white. The Norwegians would never become Americans.

For the immigration class, I researched the hard life that my great-grandfather Ellef Drægni encountered when he arrived in Minnesota. He worked near Hackensack, Minnesota, in a lumber camp. He had apprenticed as a blacksmith in Bergen, Norway, so he came over with a trade. His skill as a smith allowed him to avoid much of the backbreaking grunt work of the north woods.

For my research, my dad dug up more of Ellef's old documents and photos from the chest in our living room. In the midst of the pile was an envelope with the logo of Ellef's blacksmith shop that he eventually set up at Lake Street and Lyndale Avenue, then on the outskirts of Minneapolis. "I remember when south of Lake Street was all farms and it was almost all horses and buggies in town," my grandfather Al recalled. Now, the location is in the heart of the city, and Lake and Lyndale is a major intersection with upscale restaurants and four lanes of cars zooming by. The building where his blacksmith shop stood is gone. An asphalt parking lot fills the space surrounded by a tire dealer and Fantasy House, which advertises sex paraphernalia as "marital aids to keep your hubby happy."

Another document charts the definition of our family name. I assumed it meant "noble one" or "heir to the throne" and gave a hint of some long-lost royal lineage more noble than William the Conqueror and Rollo the Grandeur. Instead, *Drægni* means the not-quite-so-exotic "tree dragger" (either that or "muscle spasm"). Perhaps this first definition is fitting, considering my great-grandfather's job in the lumber camps.

Ellef arrived in northern Minnesota at the same time the legend of Paul Bunyan was born and first appeared in print for the Red River Lumber Company in nearby Akeley in 1914. I imagine that the blacksmith who made Paul's mighty double-bladed axe was mostly likely based on my great-grandfather, who sharpened the saws and blades for the hardy lumberjacks.

My romantic visions of the lumber camps that I gleaned from Paul Bunyan's upbeat tall tales were dispelled when I read Peg Meier's book *Bring Warm Clothes*. She quoted an upper-middle-class Anglo-American, Horace Glenn, working in the camps in 1901, who classified all Scandinavians as "Swedes." Glenn wrote, "It is only evenings when I am forced to associate with these beasts they call Swedes that I get depressed. . . . There are probably 15 white men here to 60 Swedes. . . ." Glenn didn't even consider the Scandinavians to be "white." My dad told me that my great-grandfather Ellef was a "dark Norwegian," so he could have been considered "black" by people like Glenn.

The lumberjacks "cannot utter the simplest sentence without beginning, ending and interspersing it with the most disgusting, blasphemous and useless profanity imaginable . . . when once thoroughly roused he can swear continuously for 15 minutes without the repetition of a single word." In these letters to his wife, Glenn wrote, "I might formulate a proverb out of this that 'there is more patriotism in teaching a Norwegian to wash his feet than in fighting Filipinos.'" Glenn was probably justifying his avoidance of serving during the Spanish-American War, when the United States occupied the Philippines.

Anglo-Americans like Glenn often viewed the Scandinavians as stinky subpar humans. Bathing was a matter of class because the rich usually had inside bathrooms and cleaned themselves regularly. To Glenn, civilizing these Norwegians, in effect, meant teaching them to bathe, not giving them the economic means for regular bathing.

Ellef left the camp after one year. Because of the subzero conditions in which the lumberjacks worked, they would often never change clothes the whole winter. My dad wrote me about his grandfather: "Ellef suffered from rheumatism for many years from working in cold buildings and hard, physical work. I'm sure his poor health started in the logging camps."

Ellef was eventually successful, in that he opened his own store and started a family, but that one year took its toll on his health for the rest of his days. More than ever, I wanted to see his home on the Drægni farm that he gave up for a new, perilous life in America.

"Take Everything for Good Fish"

The fishmonger at the Ravnkloa seafood shop in Trondheim tricked me. Seeing a gullible tourist, he asked me if I'd like to taste a bite of dark red fish meat called *hval* that had been marinating. Always eager to try something new, I took the slice he carved with his razor-sharp knife. I munched on a big piece that tasted more like oily, rubbery beef than cod and asked the name of the fish. "In English, it's called 'whale,'" he smirked. After that, I switched to the Fiskehallen, a less touristy fish shop, for all my fish needs.

Living next to the North Sea in Trondheim, I was determined to try all kinds of fish, but swimming mammals like whale were not on the list. I preferred herring, or the "silver of the sea," which was a required appetizer at my dad's Norwegian dinner. At the Fiskehallen, I witnessed Norwegian creativity when it comes to fish. Herring was flavored with juniper berries, *rømme* (35 percent fat sour cream), mustard dill, or red wine sauce for *matjes*. I tried in vain to convince Katy to travel to the World's Longest Herring Table in Florø, Norway, in June where a four-hundred-meter-long table extends through town and is piled high with herring.

I'd have to be content with a newfound treat: herring cakes, essentially a fried patty of ground herring, egg, and bread crumbs. I fried them in a little oil, garnished them with lemon, and served them to Katy. Her face scrunched up when she ate them. "Why would you want to mash up fish fillets into a little ball anyway?" she asked.

Our friend Inger was equally disgusted. "You ate herring cakes? Ugh! My mother once tried to save money at home, so she said we were going to eat herring for weeks. We had salt

herring and herring cakes, and now I can never eat them."
Even so, Inger gave us a jar of pickled herring for Christmas.

Pickled herring was a special treat when I was growing up,
but to many Norwegians it's considered poor food. Similarly,
in the past *torsk,* or cod, was daily fare, and the elusive salmon
was reserved for special occasions, before fish farms in the
fjords made salmon as cheap as the overfished cod. In fact,
torsk is so ordinary that a variation on the word for cod, *tosk,*
means "a common fool."

Herring, on the other hand, was responsible for fueling
naval empires in Europe because eating a couple of the fish
daily would provide enough protein for a sailor—at least that's
what my dad told me to get me to eat herring. The oily fish
were salted or cleaned and stacked tightly in a barrel of brine
with a few inches of air on the top to avoid gassy buildup and
subsequent explosions.

In the year 1549, the giant schools of herring disappeared.
The king of Denmark and Norway feared that the heavens
were punishing his sinful subjects, so he issued a proclamation:
"Since there is danger that God may withdraw his blessing on
account of the great sins and vices of inhabitants of the coasts,
our tax gatherers, each one in his own district, shall see to it
that the people in the fishing stations lead good and Christian
lives. . . ." Obedient prayer and careful obedience to the Bible
were credited with returning the herring stocks to the North
Sea a decade later.

Inger told me that the other food staple growing up was
hval. "When I was a girl, whale meat was very cheap. I do like
whale meat, but it depends how it's cooked. Sometimes it can
taste like *tran* [cod liver oil] if they don't cook it right." Even
though the Fiskehallen has large posters advertising whale
meat, I don't feel right about munching on Moby Dick.

Instead of whale, I could try the fish balls or cod tongues if
I felt adventurous. For the uninitiated, though, the fishmonger
at the Fiskehallen recommended *klippefisk,* or dried cod. "It's a

little snack that you can eat called 'Lofoten Candy,'" he said in reference to the rugged Lofoten Islands, where giant schools of cod are fished nearly to extinction.

My classmate Helen loved *klippefisk,* a sort of cod jerky. "It's mostly what children eat, though." Children? I asked. "Oh yes, they have it as a snack. I only have it about once a month now, and it reminds me of my childhood." Not to burst her bubble, I tried to hide that eating *klippefisk* seems like chewing on fishy shoe leather and that a little package I bought at Fiske-hallen gave my whole backpack the smell of the sea — I feared luring alley cats to follow me around.

I read that in spite of the value placed on fresh fish, in Norway's past, fresh food was often considered unhealthy. Meats and fish were usually salted for preservation and to kill any bacteria. Creative Norwegians either boiled, buried, dried, pickled, or soaked fish in lye. No wonder a Portuguese fish-monger in Bergen lamented, "Norway has the best fish in the world, but they don't know how to cook it. They boil it!"

I'm sure the Mediterranean countries have fantastic recipes, but I found Trondheim to be a fish-eaters' paradise with un-usual catches of the day including peppered mackerel, curried herring, smoked salmon, dried cod, and all the fresh fish imag-inable. Still, though, we hadn't found the recipe to write home about.

Perhaps in hope of avoiding bizarre Norwegian special-ties, Katy asked her midwife, Sigrid, if there were any foods she should avoid eating now that she was pregnant. "I don't think so," Sigrid responded, and Katy looked disappointed. "You can eat what you want. Well, some people say that preg-nant women shouldn't eat *rakfisk.* I don't know what it is in English, 'rotten fish'? But if you like it, though, I think it's OK."

At the Fiskehallen, I asked the fishmonger about this dangerous-sounding dish, but he said it was a delicacy only available at Christmas. Katy breathed a sigh of relief knowing she had a brief reprieve until December.

Instead, our friend Henning recommended the cured salmon. "*Gravlaks,* is similar to *rakfisk,* but better," he explained. "To make *gravlaks,* we catch the salmon, put some dill on it, and then bury it in the ground for a few days. It sounds strange, but it's very good!" He pointed out that "*grav* means 'buried,' like 'grave' in English."

Henning asked the fishmonger at the Fiskehallen where they bury their salmon. "We have a new way to make *gravlaks* now," the fishmonger replied. "We don't bury it now, so there's no risk of botulism."

Henning was obviously disappointed that his favorite food had somehow become sanitized and safer. He told us how the Swedes have the same dish, *gravlaks,* but the Norwegians add cognac for flavor and, by default, kill any unwanted microorganisms.

With Henning, we brought a half pound of *gravlaks* back to our apartment for lunch. We smothered the cured salmon in a mustard-dill sauce and washed it down with beer and aquavit; Henning seemed satisfied.

Katy began to crave the fresh taste of *gravlaks,* perhaps to please the little Norwegian baby in her belly. Pickles, ice cream, chocolate, and other pregnancy cravings were uninteresting to her; she wanted uncooked salmon. We'd finally found the best recipe for fish that somehow comforted us thousands of miles from home. We had to enjoy the *gravlaks* while we could because only in Norway would it be truly fresh.

When we compared the freshness and texture of this uncooked *gravlaks* to Japanese sushi, Henning was appalled. "No, no, no! That's just raw fish. You could get sick!" he grimaced.

I worried the first time I heard the Norwegian expression "Take everything for good fish," which means you're a gullible fool and assume that any fish is edible and fresh. I thought I was getting fresh fish at the Fiskehallen, but how could I be sure?

Truly fresh fish is highly prized in Norway. The finicky older women of Trondheim who wait patiently in line were very careful to get the best of the daily catch of cod, trout, shrimp, or halibut on display. Somehow they knew if the fish wasn't perfect, and sometimes they walked out empty-handed rather than settling for second best.

Hans Erik, a friend of Knut and Inger's, advised me that even a few hours is too long for some connoisseurs. "I know a fisherman who will only eat fish on his boat so it's the freshest possible. The first thing he does on his boat is start the water boiling. Then he throws in his line. That way, the fish is barely out of the water before it's on his plate. He won't eat fish any other way."

The Norwegian expression for such fresh cod is *"blodfersk,"* or "blood-fresh." If that was the only way to have fresh fish, I'd never had it. I resolved that I wasn't going to be a foolish *tosk* and would find the freshest fish in town. That was when I discovered a couple of fishing boats docked in downtown Trondheim every Tuesday.

Katy just wanted fresh shrimp that were cooked on board the ship. At home we would peel them and dip them in lemon and mayonnaise like the Norwegians do since we couldn't find any tangy cocktail sauce in Trondheim. Today, though, I wanted two giant fillets to grill. Obviously, my Norwegian needed some work, since he heaved his two biggest fish onto a scale, plopped them into a plastic sack, and handed the weighty load to me.

I explained that my wife and I couldn't possibly eat so much, so I asked for the smallest fish he had. He was not pleased but let me have one that was still huge for just twenty kroner, a bargain by Norwegian standards. I realized he had no intention of cleaning the fish and that my manhood would be called into question if I pushed the issue.

"So you know how to clean it, right?" Katy asked as we walked away with our booty.

"Oh sure, I've cleaned lots of fish back in Minnesota up at the lake," I replied, which was sort of true. I'd helped my grandma clean northern pike. She would whack the poor fish with a canoe paddle if they kept moving.

"What kind of fish did you buy?"

"Umm, I guess I don't know..." I replied. "But it's a beauty, isn't it? And so fresh!"

Back at the apartment, Katy read the *Herald Tribune* on the sunny balcony as I laid newspapers across the kitchen counter. I rubbed the sweat from my brow as I prepared to cut the eighteen-inch fish. The clear scales were still on and stuck to everything I touched. My knife was dull, so I had to get on top of it and lean on it with all my weight. The slippery fish slid across the wet newspapers, but after a bit of wrestling, I managed to slice it wide open. I was pulling out the entrails with my hands covered in blood when Katy walked into the kitchen.

"Jesus! What are you doing to that poor thing? That poor fish!" she yelled.

"This is dinner," I replied simply. "Perhaps it's best that you don't watch."

She just stood in the doorway and couldn't help making gagging gestures. "What do you have stuck all over your forehead?" she asked. Fish scales were stuck to my skin, and I quickly wiped them off. Fish blood was now smeared over my eyes, and Katy left the room.

After much slashing, I filleted the fish, but I couldn't imagine that most fishmongers did it in as many pieces as I did. Perhaps I could make soup or fry little fish sticks. I paged through our Norwegian cookbook for a good recipe and found the typical suggestion of boiling all the flavor out of the fish in a pot of salted water with a dash of vinegar added to hold the meat together, but that seemed like a shame for such a fresh catch. In typical Scandinavian fashion, the book proclaimed that the fish "should have no other flavor than its own" and warned against adding any spices or seasonings that would "diminish the flavor of the fish." Some would call this simply bland. I remembered the observation of my Norwegian classmate Vigdis: "You Americans are always asking, 'Does it taste fishy?' Of course it tastes fishy; it's fish!"

Instead, I found a recipe from the Lofoten Islands in the cookbook that recommended breading the fish with flour, frying it in hot oil with some butter, then pouring heavy cream over the top. At least the smell of splattering oil dispelled the raw fish smell in the kitchen.

After a good hour of fighting for our food, I triumphantly placed our beautiful fish dinner on the table along with a big salad. Katy gazed down at her plate. "Did you chop its head off?"

I didn't answer, so she finally looked up from her plate with a curious grimace in anticipation of the response. "I didn't need to chop off its head because I gutted it, stripped off the skin, and then sliced off the meat."

She winced dramatically. "I just didn't know this side of you," she said. If I was capable of slaughtering this innocent little fish, where would it all end? Katy stared at me as though trying to understand this new killer instinct in me and what kind of father I'd make.

"It's actually delicious, but you don't have to eat it if you don't want to," I said, trying to defuse the situation—never argue with a pregnant woman.

Katy picked at her fish sadly. I relished each bite of the delicious, but heavy, fish. Before we'd even finished dinner, my stomach churned violently from the combination of the cream on top of greasy fried fish. Katy smiled with an I-told-you-so look as if the fish gods were punishing me for massacring one of their own and leaving our kitchen cabinets and floors covered in the evidence. I could tell that Katy didn't believe I had a simple stomachache; this was guilt, plain and simple. Here was divine retribution for bringing a brutal slaughter home to our little apartment. After that meal, we bought our fish, already filleted, from the trustworthy souls at Fiskehallen.

A Free Upbringing

A ten-minute walk from our apartment door brought us to the Lade peninsula stretching out into the wide Trondheimfjord. It was July, so we lay down our beach towels on a bit of sand and soaked up the gentle sun. Adults were vigorously swimming in the water while kids constructed mammoth sand castles with moats and flags.

After sandwiches and a bottle of Solo orange soda, we walked down to the shoreline. Katy stepped bravely into the water and screamed, "Jesus! It's freezing!" She jumped out, refused to go swimming, and explained her theory that cold water is dangerous for pregnant women.

The water was indeed frigid, and I realized why the kids were smart enough to stay in the sand and why the adults had to swim energetic laps to stay warm. After Katy shouted, all eyes were on me to see if I'd brave the water. Rather than torturing myself with a slow entry, I ran all the way in. Once submerged, my skin was so cold that I couldn't feel when I brushed against some jellyfish, luckily not the stinging kind. My stomach, full of cheese sandwiches, tightened violently, and I quickly treaded water to avoid sinking. A healthy Norwegian swimming farther out nodded her approval, saying something about how refreshing the water was today. I didn't take time to have a conversation as I was desperately dog-paddling to shore.

Since Trondheim's fjord left us shivering, Knut and Inger suggested we take the streetcar up to the hills the next day to swim in warmer lakes. The trolley again shuddered its way up the old tracks, by a tram museum, and finally to the edge of a pristine lake. Huge pines rose above moss-covered sheets of stone that led down into the crystal-clear water. I followed a few kids who jumped off a meter-high ledge into the water.

Once again, my heart nearly stopped from the cold. "This certainly isn't like a Minnesota lake," Katy said as she dipped her feet into the water. The water came from melted snow via frigid mountain streams.

The best place for taking a dip is the downtown swimming pool on the end of the pier where the coastal steamers dock. Slightly salty water is scooped up from the fjord and—most importantly—heated for the nine different-sized indoor pools with everything from warm waterfalls to a swiftly moving "river" pool. Four-story glass windows give sweeping views of the fjord, so we could watch the Hurtigruten coastal steamers that passed daily by the island of Munkholmen.

One day, a busload of schoolkids stormed the pool. A group of boys singing a Norwegian Christmas carol, even though December was five months away, piled into the changing room as I was putting on my swimsuit. One of them chose the locker adjacent to mine, and they all decided they wanted to be right next to each other. They changed in a rush; clothes and underwear were thrown at each other in fun. Wearing goggles, they looked like identical nine-year-old boys. Some of them put on flippers and flopped around the locker room. When the inevitable chase started, the boys with the flippers stumbled when running forward, so they simply turned around to run backwards. To avoid the shock of the shower, they wet their hair in the sink, so the lifeguard wouldn't tell them to go back and bathe.

I was witnessing what my Norwegian teacher, Sissel, told me was *en fri oppdragelse,* a free upbringing in which children are allowed to roam and to express themselves. She had told me, "My husband is English, and when we were trying to decide where to raise our kids, it was very obvious that Norway is much more friendly." She continued, "In England they really like to punish their kids. Norway, on the other hand, is a paradise for children." In fact, I'd often seen young kids out playing or walking down the sidewalk with no adult supervision.

Another student, Shannon, who was a Norwegian Canadian mother, differed, "The 'free-upbringing' basically means that kids can do anything they damn please. Sometimes they're a bunch of animals. I just wonder how they'll be when they grow up. At the same time, it is a kind of paradise to have children here since it's so kid friendly. They're just part of everyday life here."

Fully aware that very soon I would have a little boy of my own, I watched as these boys did whatever they pleased and the teachers barely noticed their mischief.

Katy was waiting outside the men's room for me and had to dodge this band of boys walking in reverse bumping into everyone. She told me, "In the showers, I looked down, and there was this whole group of little girls just staring at me and my pregnant belly. All I could do was say, 'Hi.' I suppose they were all thinking, 'Is that what's going to happen to me someday?'"

Touching Katy's protruding belly, I could feel our little boy kicking and rolling around. An active little man.

The gaggle of boys was busy scurrying up the ladder to the four levels of diving platforms. A lifeguard stood at the first level, I assumed to stop swimmers from using the highest platform. No, he was just keeping an eye on the pool to ensure that no one landed on anyone's head. Most of the boys were thrilled to attempt ill-fated flips from the ten-foot-high diving board, but some didn't want to waste their time, and they headed for the frightening seventy-foot high dive to jump off in pairs. The four seconds of air time gave them a chance to contemplate their fate before smashing into the water. The boys jumped only once.

In the large whirlpool, some of the boys played catch with a big foam cube that was obviously hard to control. When it bonked an older man on the head, he uttered, "*Uff da!*" (Ouch) but didn't say anything to the culprits. No one, including the lifeguards, reprimanded the boys or even gave them a warning look. In a way, I think the lifeguards wished they could be so young and carefree. Who would want to spoil these boys' childhood and look like a miserly curmudgeon? This was the essence of a free upbringing: adults wanted to see children have the happy childhood that perhaps they didn't have themselves. Here at the pool, a free upbringing meant that teachers got a much-deserved break in the beach chairs. Everyone won.

Four loud musical notes sounded over the intercom, and a crackly voice made an announcement: the wave pool was now open. The kids shrieked with excitement and hopped to their feet. They grabbed their kickboards and used them as surfboards as the waves hit. The boards sank under their feet and then shot up into the air as others ducked. A new game of launching kickboards ensued amid the chaos of the crashing waves. Katy and I could sit in the whirlpool and watch the kickboard competition without being thumped on the head. We still had a few years before our boy would be big enough to create such a ruckus.

When the boys stopped for lunch, I thought I had a break from the racket. Then a small cup of ketchup flew over the edge of the café's veranda and splattered on the floor in front of me. My legs looked like I had just butchered a cow. Before a lifeguard thought I had a giant open wound and kicked me out, I stepped into a bathroom to wash it off.

When I came out, a pool employee circled the edge of the pool with long white rubber gloves, a little net, and a bucket. "I think she's looking for floaters," Katy told me. "One of the little kids didn't get to the bathroom in time, so it's time to go now."

The showers were quiet until the boys entered. The showerheads were wielded as weapons until some used a cup, then a bucket for superior firepower. One kid dumped his whole bottle of shampoo over his head to cover his entire body in suds. The bubbles were thrown at the other kids.

The boys peed in pairs and had a yellow swordfight over the toilet. When I walked by their stall with the open door, one of the boys turned around midstream and sprinkled the other boy's leg. "*Oy!*" screamed the surprised boy with the wet leg as they both ran back to the showers. The pool staff hosed down the toilets daily.

One of the boys tied the end of his towel around his neck like a cape and declared himself king of Norway. Another boy wrapped his towel around his head like a turban to be the queen, but his towel fell into a puddle in the shower. The resourceful boy used one of the hair dryers to dry off his entire body. When the other boys saw the hair dryers, they blew their hair up into oversized pompadours and admired themselves in the mirror as they sang into their hairbrushes.

A boy with a camera in his bag started shooting pictures of the scene, oblivious that most of them weren't wearing clothes. None of the boys seemed to notice they were naked until a father brought his six-year-old girl into the room. Suddenly, the boys were quiet and orderly. They quickly and self-consciously got dressed by their lockers. Annoyed, some of them looked nervously at the little girl, who didn't even notice them but was happily putting on her little flower bikini.

Columbus Was Norwegian

"Leif Ericson?" asked Xavier, a French Ph.D. student in my Norwegian class. "I've never heard of him. Was he some sort of king?"

We were sharing our Norwegian textbook that featured a heroic painting of Leif Ericson in front of his Viking ship landing in Vinland. The text proudly declared him as the discoverer of America in AD 1000, and no mention was even made of Columbus. "Is this true? How can this be?" Xavier asked.

My Norwegian friend Knut was disgusted. "I just wonder what they teach them in France," he responded. I pointed out to Knut that Leif Ericson wasn't really Norwegian because he was born in Iceland. Leif's father, Eric the Red, was banished from Norway for murder.

"Oh, that doesn't matter. Iceland was a Norwegian colony, and they were all Vikings," Knut said.

Another classmate, Sophie, from the Nordfjord told me about a book that proved that Columbus was a Norwegian from her area of the country. "What?" I responded. "Now Norway is even claiming that Columbus himself was from here?" I'd heard that some suggested that Columbus might have been Spanish rather than Italian, but Norwegian?

In the university library, I found many copies of the book *Christopher Columbus — en Europeer fra Norge?* (Christopher Columbus — a European from Norway?). Norwegian author Tor Borch Sannes pointed out that Columbus gathered his knowledge about the New World from his early trip to Norway in 1477, and that Columbus's coat of arms was identical to that of a Norwegian family's from the Nordfjord. According to Sannes, Columbus had blond hair and blue eyes and was really named "Christopher Bonde" from the town of Hyen, just north of the Sognefjord.

I brought a copy to Xavier, who paged through it in disbelief, "Now I can't believe any of these Norwegian claims. I could just as easily say that Lafayette discovered America."

I wanted to find out more about this theory, so I called the publisher of *Christopher Columbus — en Europeer fra Norge?* to interview the author. "We haven't heard from Sannes for about seven years," the publisher told me mysteriously. "He moved to one of those — as we say in Norway — 'low-price' or 'discount' countries like Romania or Argentina."

My friend Knut just laughed at the obvious Norwegian pride of the author that clouded his judgment. "We discovered America not just once, but twice!" he joked.

On the Meat Bus

Meat is expensive in Norway (a Burger King Whopper sets you back ten bucks). Because of the prices, Swedish stores pay for a bus to bring pensioners, especially little old ladies, over the border to do their shopping. Which is how Katy and I found ourselves in a line of senior citizens waiting for the meat bus. When the unmarked bus pulled up, the ladies hurriedly piled in through both the front and rear doors. I asked the driver if this was the bus to Sweden. "Ya, ya. Please enter," he replied mechanically, as though he couldn't wait to get on the road.

As soon as the bus was full, everyone immediately pulled out cinnamon rolls or knitting needles and began to chat. A woman in front of us managed to eat a sandwich, knit an entire sock, and carry on a conversation simultaneously. When she found out we were from Minnesota, she asked, "I have relatives in Richfield; do you know them?"

I felt a tap on my shoulder from a pair of women behind us who were excited that a young couple had joined their group. They took us under their wing after I explained that we needed to shop in Sweden because my wife was pregnant. "Oh yes, we can tell. She must eat."

Katy didn't seem pleased that our mission was just to fatten her up. "Will we understand anyone in Sweden?" she asked. The women assured us that the Swedish storekeepers understand Norwegian, which didn't help us much. Do they take Norsk money? "Oh *ja!*"

They asked us, "Did you order your wine or alcohol ahead? No? Here's the phone number for next time."

As we passed through the tunnel by the town of Hell and by more moose-crossing signs than we could count, the bus driver cracked jokes and did impersonations over the micro-

phone, all the while steering the bus around hairpin mountain turns. The little old ladies stopped their knitting to laugh
in unison.

After two hours of traveling on a small one-lane road, the
bus crossed over into Sweden. No one asked for our passports
at the border; the guard waved the meat bus through. The bus
driver pointed out a Swedish sign that said *tull*, or toll. The
women laughed heartily, and one of the knitters explained that
it meant "nonsense" in Norwegian. Rather than going through
the toll booth, the bus went to the store. We expected to see a
huge shopping center, but the bus pulled up to a desolate gravel
parking lot in front of a grocery store the size of a bloated
fishing shack. Now we could tell friends back home that
we'd been to Sweden and it was just desolate highlands with a
supermarket.

When the bus came to a halt and the cloud of road dust
settled, the driver teased the passengers by asking over the
intercom if everyone would buy a lot. A chorus of "*Ja!*" responded as he opened both doors. The ladies piled off in a mad
dash for the shopping carts; the calm courtesy of the bus had
disappeared. The doors of the store slid open, and in rushed
more than thirty shopping carts waiting to be filled. The surprised shopkeepers backed away as the phalanx of women
stormed the store, banging their carts against each other like
berserkers in search of a bargain.

In the madness, Katy and I lost sight of our two helpers
and were left to fend for ourselves amid the onslaught. A
butcher brought out a box of salamis two feet long and was
surrounded like a quarterback in a football huddle. The ladies
grabbed the hunks of meat right out of the cardboard container
before the butcher could put them into the refrigerator case. I
caught sight of one of our friends, who clutched a salami, held
it up to me as a trophy, and yelled, "*Kjøtt!*" (meat).

After our friends snatched the meat, I asked what the
deals of the day were. "Everything! It is all cheaper here!" one
of them told me as she struggled with her meat-laden grocery

basket. A woman walked by through the narrow aisles pushing two shopping carts loaded with whole chickens.

In spite of all the fervor, most women bought suspiciously little. "The bus comes every day, except for Sunday, of course," one of our friends explained.

The hour stop at the store was up, and the bus driver threatened to leave without us. The stowage compartment under the bus was jammed with identical plastic shopping bags tied on top. Somehow everyone knew whose sack was whose when the Norwegian border patrol made a halfhearted attempt to search the bags. Along a thousand-mile mountainous border with Sweden, crafty smugglers had to be able to sneak through somehow. Rummaging through sacks of frozen meat belonging to little old ladies was surely not what these guards had in mind when they signed up to protect Norway.

Back on the bus, the driver cracked more jokes—perhaps the same ones every day—but got giggles nevertheless. He then announced that we would stop for coffee and waffles. A loud "Hurrah!" erupted.

The bus pulled into a rest stop that looked more like a hunters' lodge, high on the mountains overlooking the pine-filled valley below. We sat down for fresh waffles smothered in cream and strawberry jam, and the women kept offering Katy more to eat. She politely declined, and they were obviously disappointed.

"Shall we see you next Friday?" one of the women asked us. "We go every Friday."

"I'm due any day, so we're not sure," Katy explained.

They perked up when I assured them we'd take the meat bus once the baby arrived.

One of them looked into our sack of Swedish groceries and asked, "What will you eat for dinner tonight?"

Before I could respond, the other woman yelled, "Meat!"

Bargain Babies

In downtown Trondheim, we went to the *trygdekontor* (insurance office) to register Katy for health care to cover the birth. The woman at the desk looked over our documents somberly and said she didn't think we qualified. We panicked.

"Oh, the government shall pay for the birth," she assured us. "I just don't know if you are eligible for maternity benefit."

I couldn't believe we'd be paid to have a baby in Norway, so I scoured the literature from the insurance office. If Katy had been working for at least six months in Norway, she would get forty-two weeks off of work at full pay or fifty-two weeks at 80 percent of her salary. Four of these weeks, however, were reserved for the husband, and if he didn't use the time, they lost that month. The forty-two or fifty-two weeks could also be divvied up between the parents, and the mother even earned vacation time from the maternity leave. The next year could be taken off without pay, but the mother still held on to her job. An extra three (and up to twelve) weeks could be taken *before* the due date. Self-employed workers as well could get 100 percent of their pay for forty-two weeks based on the past three years, and even adoption got you thirty-nine weeks of full pay or forty-nine weeks at 80 percent. If the mother wasn't working in Norway — as was our case — she'd receive a lump sum of 33,584 Norwegian kroner (about $5,000) for the baby. This sounded huge, but Norway was also the most expensive country in the world.

I told Rachel we'd feel guilty getting this benefit, but she rebutted, "Why should you feel 'guilty' about receiving money from the government? It's our money after all; even you pay taxes here now. Everyone receives the child credit, even the king does and Prince Haakon will when [his wife] Mette-Marit has her new child. After all, it's not really your money, it belongs to the baby."

No wonder I'd overheard expatriates talk about having "bargain babies" in Norway. We soon realized why the Norwegian government helps families raise their children: Prices are astronomical. "Baby buggies can cost a thousand dollars in Norway, but they'll last you a lifetime," Rachel advised us. Why would we need a stroller to last our whole life? We didn't need to spring for a super-stroller because we had lugged a simple one from Minnesota. Norwegian prams, however, had rugged eight-inch wheels to climb over snowdrifts, complete coverage for the worst blizzard, and shock absorbers so the baby Viking wouldn't feel a thing. Common courtesy called for any able-bodied passenger to help load the huge strollers on and off the buses as the coddled infants looked on at the good service.

To give new mothers a chance to get out of the house, the cinemas in Trondheim offer "Baby Kino," baby cinema. I couldn't understand why newborns would want to watch movies, but I understood when I poked my head into a showing. The show was for the moms. The entrance to the theater was jammed with dozens of empty strollers, and the lights were kept half on so no one tripped. Mothers relaxed in the comfortable chairs as the sound of slurping babies breastfeeding filled in any silence during the movie soundtrack.

Because these buggies were so big, a local café, Erichsen Konditori, announced it would no longer allow baby carriages inside. The sleeping children in their carriages had to wait outside. Apparently, leaving bundled infants in strollers outside a store while shopping inside was common in Scandinavia. I told Sissel, my Norwegian teacher, that this would never happen in the U.S. "Why not?" she asked. "What are you afraid of?" In fact, a Danish woman was arrested in Manhattan the year before for trusting New Yorkers not to snatch her baby left outside while she was inside a café.

Knut told me about a Norwegian mother who was used to the big city of Oslo and vacationed in Lærdal on the Sognefjord, where my great-grandfather came from. The mother "struggled to get the stroller through the doors of a store," Knut said. "She got strange looks from the locals. At last one of the ladies in the store cried out in indignation, 'We do not steal babies in Lærdal! The baby can stay outside.'" All these stories stand in contrast to the warning on our American stroller: "NEVER LEAVE THE CHILD UNATTENDED!"

My first reaction to this trusting instinct was that it endangered the children, but I learned that the Norwegian childcare system was the envy of much of the world. The preschools, or *barnehager,* are considered some of the best, and many of the schools have a clinic, or *helsestasjon* (health station), for the children in the neighborhood. Pediatricians travel around to these health stations once a week for checkups. Each health station has meetings for mothers with newborns to get together and chat over coffee about the problems and joys of parenting.

Not only did the Norwegian insurance system help make us financially solvent with the $5,000 to help raise our impending baby, it would automatically deposit 972 Norwegian kroner (about $145) into our bank account every month. This money, which was doubled if you were a single parent, was to encourage families to have babies and stop the negative birth rate. It would help raise our child and would be continued until he was eighteen years of age or until we left Norway.

A brochure put out by the Norwegian National Insurance Administration clarified this welfare policy of pure socialism for the advantage of families: "Child benefit is to help cover expenses related to having a child/children. It is also a redistributive device between families with children and those without and is intended mainly to even out differences in income to the advantage of families with children."

Knut explained that "it's not pure charity. Because the welfare system is founded on taxation, it's vital to produce taxpayers to secure the system's foundation of a stable birthrate and give the double-working households the possibility to have children without too much economic or career risk. Italy and England haven't managed this, and the birthrate is too low, and the welfare system is at risk."

Astrid, a classmate and single mom, weighed in, "I heard that people in the United States are embarrassed to take money from the government. What do they call it—welfare? Is this true? I'm not ashamed because that is what it's there for, to help children."

Earth Mothers at the Sick House

We had it all figured out. We would not be like the movies, when the panicked father has to race to the hospital through red lights with his wife screaming and then giving birth in the waiting room. No. We would casually saunter in, and Katy could give birth just like she was having an eye exam.

The big, impersonal Saint Olav's hospital in Trondheim didn't offer water births, and Katy dreamed of giving birth in a large, warm tub so the baby could be born underwater. Katy didn't want any drugs, so the bath would relieve any pain. The baby wouldn't be breathing yet, so the transition from warm womb to warm water would be soothing for mother and baby. "You must talk to Sigrid in Orkanger," the receptionist at St. Olav's told us. "She's the only one who will do that around here."

This complicated our plan for the birth, as Orkanger was an hour away by bus. We remained calm, though, and practiced the trip many times so Katy could see her midwife, Sigrid. When the baby decided it was time to come, we'd just board the bus for a relaxing hour trip along the fjord to Orkanger, a town of red wooden houses.

"The bus? You're going to take the bus?" asked Katy's mom, a nurse.

"Sure," responded Katy confidently. "It's better than sitting in some taxi where you can't move around for an hour. They say it's good to walk once you know the baby is coming, so we'll just walk down to the station and hop on a bus. It'll be fine." Maybe the bus wouldn't be as fast as driving, but we'd heard terrible stories of women in labor for forty-eight hours, so why not spend the first hour on a scenic drive through rural Norway?

Sigrid the midwife, or *jordmor,* at the Orkdal Sykehus, or "sick house," had told us not to worry. "Many women live across the fjord, and ferries are delayed when they must wait for the pregnant woman to travel down the mountains by car. This is Norway and not everyone lives close to a hospital."

The *jordmor* succeeded in calming us so much about the birth that we even planned a trip to Bodø to visit relatives eleven hours north of Trondheim above the Arctic Circle. "Oh, Bodø," Eli, one of the *jordmødre,* said nodding her head, "I went there myself in the last month. You still have two weeks until the birth, and you can't just sit around and wait. It's fine as long as you're on the train so you can keep your feet elevated."

"Really? You don't think it's a problem that I'm pregnant?" Katy asked.

"Just go!" Eli responded. "The train passes many towns along the way. If the baby decides to come, the train can stop and let you off. They can't really do that with a plane . . ."

I was convinced; Katy wasn't. She did not want to give birth in an unknown town in the Arctic where we didn't know anyone and didn't speak the language. My suggestion that it was the doctor's orders didn't sway her. We canceled our tickets.

In its place, we signed up for a birthing class at the Orkdal Sykehus. I braced myself for couples acting out excruciating birth with heavy breathing and gruesome labor videos of shrieking mothers. Instead, Katy and I sat down around the table with other expectant couples, and Eli, the *jordmor,* offered us coffee, tea, and pastries. "How do you like Norway so far?" another couple asked us. For the first half hour, Eli and the group wanted to hear how two Americans ended up in Trondheim.

Eli asked why doctors perform so many cesarean sections in the U.S. We explained that American newspapers write that doctors often scheduled C-sections so they could fit in as many operations as possible—and not be woken up in the middle of the night. Doctors also perform the operation when there is the slightest bit of danger for the mother or baby because they could get sued. "Americans! It is crazy!" was all Eli said as she offered more sweet rolls.

Katy mentioned to Eli that she wanted to do the birth without drugs, if possible. "You can do whatever you want," Eli responded. "In the old days, we didn't have a chance to take any medication," she said. "The doctors told us, 'You got it in there, now shut your mouth and get it out!'"

We thought the whole two-hour class was going to be a carefree coffee klatch, when Eli decided we should tour the midwives' maternity wing of the hospital. Far from being an antiseptic institution, the birthing rooms had a couch, a large bathtub, and homey wooden furniture. The waiting room had plush red plaid couches, Lego tables with visiting children hard at work, and hot coffee or cocoa for anyone who stopped by. Each patient's room had a desk, a large double bed, and a table and chairs — obviously new mothers were encouraged to stay a while. Any view out the windows framed the mountains covered with maple and oak trees turning orange, red, and yellow like a hillside on fire.

The birthing class ended with Katy and the other pregnant women taking a swim in a warm therapeutic pool to relieve their pain and feel the weightlessness of the water, while the husbands ate more cookies and discussed our wives' bizarre cravings for fish in the middle of the night.

A week passed with still no sign of the baby. My mother was waiting back in Minnesota for a telephone call to tell her to come to Norway to help. She couldn't wait and came over right away.

Another week passed, and the due date arrived. We took the bus to Orkanger for a checkup with Sigrid. Katy had lost the soulful glow that pregnant women often have; she just wanted to sleep. "I just want to get this baby out of me!" she told Sigrid desperately. Sigrid explained that the due date was just an estimate and often women will go a week or two after the date. "Go home and have a good cry. The baby will come when it's ready."

We rode the bus home solemnly. I tried to cheer her up by telling her that this time next week we'd have a baby. "You don't know that!" she shot back. "This baby is never coming out. How would you like to carry a thirty-pound sack of potatoes around in your belly that forces you to pee every ten minutes?"

I stayed mum, and the steady purr of the bus's diesel engine lulled Katy to sleep.

Katy's water broke that night, October 28th, at 11:10 p.m., and the last bus had already left for the night. I had just fallen asleep. When Katy woke my mom and me, I was in a daze.

"I just need a little time to wake up," I muttered as if I could just hit the snooze button.

"Oh no you don't! You need to call the hospital right now," Katy insisted.

"Ah. Okay. Can't you just give me a minute?"

"Here's their number. Tell them we're on our way."

I obeyed and dialed. I was too tired to manage any Norwegian, so I spoke in English, "I'm calling because my wife Katy McCarthy has been a patient there, and we'd like to come in now..."

"Wait," the nurse cut me off. I heard her looking through some papers. "How do you spell her name?" I spelled it. "No, she is not a patient here. I'm sorry. Bye-bye."

"Wait, wait!" I said before she could hang up. "Yes, she is and wants to come in right now to have a baby."

"No, she isn't here now. I'm sorry."

"Yes, but she wants to come in there and have the baby there right now!"

"Oh, I see."

"Her water has broken."

"Yes. Then she must have the baby."

Now we were getting somewhere, I thought.

"Where do you live?" she continued.

"We live in Trondheim."

"OK. You must go to Saint Olav Hospital in Trondheim for a checkup."

"What? A checkup? We were told we could come to the Orkdal Sykehus to have the baby."

"No. If you live in Trondheim, you must go to Saint Olav," and she prepared to give me the phone number. I told her that we were coming to Orkdal.

"Why do you want to come to Orkdal when Saint Olav Hospital is so near?"

I was beginning to think this was one of those never-ending anxiety dreams. "We had all our appointments in Orkdal with Sigrid, and Katy wants to have a water birth."

"Oh, then you shall come to Orkdal," she said finally. "We shall see you soon. Bye-bye." She hung up.

Katy asked, "What on earth was that all about? No, don't tell me! Quick, call a cab."

I dialed the eight-digit number for the taxi. An answering machine responded in Norwegian, and I didn't understand a word. I called back three more times to decipher the message. "What is it?" Katy asked anxiously.

"They're closed," I replied.

"What? How can that be?"

"Well, they gave another number that is only five digits — 07373 — but that can't be right," I replied.

Katy gave me a desperate look, and I imagined that I was going to have to deliver the baby at home after all. No, she wants a water birth, and there are dirty dishes in the sink, I thought.

I searched the apartment for a phone book. What do I do? After all the fuss we'd gone through to get phone books from Telenor, and then I couldn't find them. After looking everywhere, Katy remembered the phone books were under her mattress to elevate her feet to keep them from swelling.

Skipping through the white pages, pink pages, and blue pages, I opened the yellow pages to "Taxi" but found nothing.

Isn't the word "taxi" international, like Coca-Cola and shampoo? "Get the dictionary!" I said. "How do you say 'taxi cab' in Norwegian?"

Katy looked at me in disbelief. All my Norwegian lessons—and me, for that matter—were worthless. She pulled the dictionary out from under her mattress. "*Drosje!*" she yelled. I found *drosjer* in the phone book, but the first number gave me another answering machine.

After many rings at the second number, a real human answered who spoke English. "Oh no, we don't send out taxis at night. You need to call TrønderTaxi at 07373." I didn't dare tell Katy that this was the original number I didn't think was correct.

"This is such an adventure!" my mom said excitedly. Katy and I looked at each other exasperated.

The taxi arrived in less than five minutes, and we loaded everything. "Let's try not to tell him that I'm going to give birth and that my water broke," Katy whispered to me because she didn't want him to get nervous while driving and have an accident.

"You want to go all the way to Orkdal?" the taxi driver asked. "Are you having a baby?"

Katy and I slunk low in our seat; the game was up. The driver seemed glad to be entrusted with such an important mission.

While Katy and I sat anxiously in the backseat, my mom chatted happily with the driver about all the great things to see in Trondheim. I realized I only had about the equivalent of $20 in my pocket—not nearly enough for an hour-long cab ride. He wouldn't just leave us out here, would he? Should I just be quiet until the end of the ride and then at least we'd be at the hospital?

"I'm sorry, but you know this will be a very expensive ride—maybe $150—because it's night rates," he warned, as I began to sweat thinking that maybe he'd want to be paid up front. "We do take credit cards, if you don't have enough kroner." And I breathed easily for the moment.

He let us off at the *sykehus* in Orkdal, and the *jordmor* examined Katy. "You are only dilated to one centimeter, so you have some time," she told Katy. "Why don't you get some rest?"

"That's a great idea," I concurred. "Let's get some sleep."

"Sleep? How can you think about sleep when I'm going to have a baby!?" Katy exclaimed.

The *jordmor* gave Katy an enormous diaper to wear to stop any discharge, and I lay down on the couch and fell fast asleep. My mom spent the night in the waiting room. After a couple of hours, Katy woke me. "We've got to do something! I can't stand it anymore!" she said.

The *jordmor* calmly entered the room and told Katy to relax. "Relax? How can I relax when I feel like my back is breaking?" I gave Katy a massage but that didn't help.

The *jordmor* hooked wires up to Katy that ran to a fetal monitor. The display showed that the baby's heart rate wasn't bouncing back after contractions. "I'm sorry, but we can't do a water birth," she said trying to mask her concern.

"OK," said Katy. "Then give me an epidural and fast!"

The *jordmor* phoned the anesthesiologist at home. In spite of the early hour, he came in, a suit and tie on under his scrubs. Within minutes, Katy was feeling better, and finally we slept.

A new *jordmor*, Karin, woke us at 8 a.m. to check the fetal monitor. "By the way," she told me, "the breakfast cart has arrived if you're hungry."

Katy winced at the idea of food, but she said I could go. By this time, my mother had woken up as well from her night on the waiting room couch. We loaded our trays with hot coffee and thick cream and breakfast sandwiches of cucumbers, tomatoes, and Jarlsberg cheese. Rather than sit in some lonely cafeteria while Katy was in labor, we brought our breakfast into the delivery room to keep her company.

As we munched our sandwiches at a little table at the foot of Katy's bed, she looked up in disbelief that we were eating. "Um, you know, there's going to be some really gross stuff happening here soon, and you have a front-row seat." Embarrassed, we stopped eating and moved over to the couch on the side.

Karin, the *jordmor*, however, scooted the table laden with our sandwiches over to us on the couch. Katy groaned.

Seeing our drinks, Karin said, "I think I'll get some coffee as well. Would you like a refill?"

"Doesn't anyone realize that I'm going to have a baby?" Katy said as the rest of us sipped hot coffee.

"All we can do now is wait," the *jordmor* said. She explained that the epidural drugs had to wear off so Katy could feel the pain and push properly. I didn't understand why they gave her a pain reliever only to let it wear off, but I think they wanted her to dilate. The fetal monitor wasn't giving the proper readings, so Karin called another *jordmor* and a doctor. A tall woman atop stiletto heels with lush dark red hair swirled into a bun entered the room. She was the obstetrician and spoke only Norwegian with a thick German accent. Karin the *jordmor* ran the show, though, and spoke nearly perfect English. Sometimes she searched for words. "Please Katy. Can you move your, how do you say, 'ass'? Can you move your ass?"

As the contractions came more regularly, I expected Katy to scream, but she seemed to internalize the pain and use it to push. The midwives and doctor jumped to action and prepared all the towels and monitors. A tray of surgical tools on a dolly was wheeled close to the bed. Now, it was up to Katy.

The German doctor spoke with a two-range voice that either rose into a high falsetto or sank into a low baritone. She spoke to Katy seriously in her Germanic Norwegian, and I couldn't understand a word. Somehow in the heat of the moment, Katy understood everything and nodded. Her repressed yells seemed therapeutic, and when she hesitated, Karin encouraged her to keep going. All the while, the crew kept a watchful eye on the fetal monitor.

Katy seemed like she was going to burst as her face reddened with each push. Finally, the baby appeared. With just his purple head out, the *jordmor* quickly put two clamps on the umbilical cord that was wrapped around the baby's neck twice and cut between them. Our baby was freed from the noose of an umbilical cord entangled around his jugular. This was why the midwives had rejected the water birth and worried that his heart rate wasn't bouncing back after contractions. In the U.S., doctors would have insisted on a cesarean section to have as little risk as possible—and out of fear of a lawsuit. Yet the Norwegian midwives opted for a natural birth. Their prompt maneuvers saved our baby from strangling from the cord that had been his lifeblood. Now he was separated from his mother but still not out. Karin grabbed his little head and twisted it hard to one side to get his shoulders through. As Katy pushed with one last, long scream, Karin yanked the baby free. Involuntarily, I shouted, "Hurray! You did it!" And Katy sat back in the bed exhausted but exhilarated.

Karin quickly cleaned up the blood around the cone-headed infant and handed him to his mother. Katy held her baby for the first time. "My baby!" she gasped happily through her exhaustion.

Karin only let Katy hold him for a minute as she had to remove any liquid from his lungs and make sure he was breathing properly. I came with Karin to help weigh and measure the little blue baby who was no bigger than a football. I tried to imagine how this little boy would change our lives as we watched him grow, but now Karin had to bring our baby with his full head of dark hair to an incubator for two hours to warm him and make sure the nooselike umbilical cord hadn't caused any damage.

Katy was worn out but relieved. "All I need is sleep," she said, as we went into our large family room with a big double bed and a small wooden cradle.

A few hours later, Karin knocked at the door carrying our swaddled baby. I prepared the little cradle for him to lie down, but she stopped me. "No, no. The baby belongs here," she said and pointed to the middle of our double bed. "The baby sleeps between you." We thought of all those terrible stories about parents rolling over on their babies during the middle of night. The *jordmor* knew best, though, and we were too tired to argue. Our little baby the size of a warm loaf of bread snuggled up between Katy and me and fell sound asleep.

The Name of the Devil

"Give him a good Norwegian name!" insisted the *jordmor*. "I know it seems strange to give him a big grown-up name, but you have to remember that he will someday be an old man with hair sticking out his ears and nose. He will someday be a great-grandfather, and you can't have him with a baby's name!"

She said, "I recognized your name, 'Drægni,' from the Lusterfjord. That's right, isn't it? I worked there for years in Lærdal. The people are very different. In Trondheim, maybe because there are not such big mountains, the people are more open and friendly. In Luster, the people are more closed, perhaps because of the nearly vertical fjells closing them in. The people there are very funny, though. They have a unique sense of humor and aren't afraid to make a little fun of themselves."

Because of this, we considered the name "Loke," the trickster Norwegian god. Our friend Knut was shocked, "What? That's the devil. I know that even some Norwegian parents name their child 'Loke,' but imagine calling to your child on the playground, 'Here Satan!'"

My mother suggested "Snorre" after the first Norwegian baby born in America, but that sounds too much like the little-known eighth dwarf who snores. Ole, Bjørn, and Thor are all overused. Many other popular names don't translate well into English. The Swedish "Sven" is "Svein" in Norwegian but pronounced too close to "swine," "Petter" is no good, "Dag" is pronounced "dog," "Odd" just isn't fair for a baby, and "Simon" is pronounced "semen."

After consulting lists of names, we finally settled on "Eilif" after my great-grandfather from the Sognefjord. My great-grandfather spelled his name five different ways on documents, so we opted for the version that would be pronounced correctly by both Norwegians and Americans. The *jordmor* approved.

"Eilif is a good Norwegian name. We have three Eilifs in my family and three more in my daughter-in-law's family, and they all spell it differently. Eilif, Eilov. . . That doesn't matter, though, because it's all the same name. His name must be approved by the government now." Approved? "Yes, it shouldn't be a problem. They now even accept most foreign names."

Ironically, with all this hospitality and after the Norwegian government had invested so much in making sure our son is taken care of, he couldn't get Norwegian citizenship because both Katy and I are American.

We asked Sigrid if we should have Eilif circumcised.

"No!" she responded, shocked. "Why would you do that? You're not Jewish, are you? You don't do that in the America, do you? Isn't it only for religious reasons?"

After the birth, we were given a large room for the three of us with three meals a day (plus a snack and late-evening soup) delivered right outside the room. Many of the mothers, though, preferred that their husbands stay at home, so they could form a sort of girls' club while pushing their babies around the hospital in their little beds on wheels.

The midwives told us that we should stay at least three or four days in our family room to make sure that the breast-feeding was going well. In this large room with a view of the snow-capped mountains and meals delivered, why would we leave? We asked the head midwife, Sigrid, if they ever have trouble with mothers who won't leave the hospital. She told us, "Sometimes if we have too many people having babies, we have to ask mothers who have been here for a long time, 'So, how are things going? Do you have any plans?'"

On the fourth day when they served us a dinner of *risegrøt* (heavy rice porridge smothered in butter) with hard salami, we took it as a hint that our time was up.

We prepared to take the bus back to Trondheim, but the midwives wouldn't hear of it. The government health insurance would pay for our hour-long taxi drive and even reimburse us 90 percent of the cab fare we had paid to get to the hospital.

Mørketid: The Dark Time

By the time we were back in our apartment, the first snowflakes had found their way to the ground. In our neighborhood of Lademoen, green grass pushed through the dusting of snow, but the hills above Trondheim, where my classes were held, had nearly six inches of powder. "Ya, it's a little early, but I do love to ski," my classmate Vigdis told me.

I asked another classmate, Astrid, if now was when we should start drinking for the long winter. "Oh no!" she joked. "We start in the summer because then we can sit outside and enjoy the warm weather."

Katy didn't share my excitement for such an early snow because our apartment was already cold. The only heat for all the rooms was two small electric radiators and a woodstove, for which we had no fuel. To keep the living room warm, I told Katy that I would order wood for the metal stove in the apartment when I came back from a weekend in Oslo, but she couldn't wait. By the time I arrived home, she had carried a cord of wood up the three flights of stairs — with the baby in a sling — to our apartment. She was not happy to lug the wood by herself, but at least she had a roaring fire thanks to the pile of wood filling our living room.

Still, our bedroom was freezing cold, so we called our landlord, Arne, to grumble and ask if he could put in an electric radiator. "No, no," he replied.

I was surprised because he and his wife, Oddbjørg, had never refused any request we had made and had bought us anything we needed for the apartment. I knew it wasn't the money, so perhaps he misunderstood me. I asked again, "Do you think we could get an electric heater for the bedroom?"

"No, no. We like it cold. You don't want to sleep with it hot, do you? It's best cold."

I told him that we could see our breath in the bedroom, so we'd just like it a little warmer.

"You do? You want to sleep with it warm? Why?" he seemed perplexed.

"Well, we think it's too cold for a newborn," I explained.

"Ah, I see. If you think it's best, then I will buy a heater for you," he said, and I could tell he thought this was a terrible idea. Arne explained that the cold was healthier, especially for sleeping. Along with other Norwegian friends, Arne suggested we bundle up our baby, Eilif, and leave him outside on the balcony so he'd sleep better.

Katy laughed at this suggestion, but we saw how the cold weather knocked out Eilif when we put him in the stroller. To test Arne's theory, Eilif was our guinea pig. Katy wrapped blankets around him, fastened a hat on his little head, and placed him out on the snowy balcony in the frigid Norwegian weather. We didn't hear another peep for an hour, but he seemed to still be breathing. After the second hour, we panicked that he was frozen solid, so we woke him out of his deep, deep sleep. He woke up just long enough to eat and then returned to his Norwegian hibernation.

The Norwegian saying "You always have to keep your fate in front of you" went through my mind as I held Eilif and looked out our apartment window at the cemetery across the street. The field of tombstones shimmered all night with the lights from hundreds of candles to keep away the inevitable darkness. This was All Saints' Day, and the parking lot was jammed as dozens of Norwegians entered the cemetery carrying flowers and candles in search of the snow-covered graves of their relatives and friends. Many stayed in the graveyard for hours, holding vigil and sipping hot chocolate from shiny metal thermoses.

Now that we were back in our apartment, my mom prepared a welcome-home cake for the occasion. A "Happy Birthday" banner of cut-out letters carried a double meaning because today was also her birthday. Eilif slept through his party. In fact, he slept most of the time.

"I think you've got one of those perfect babies," my mom said.

I shrugged and responded, "Isn't that what babies do? Sleep?" I thought that being a father wouldn't be so hard after all.

My mother was content that Katy and I were going to make it as new parents. After helping us get on our feet, she packed up her suitcase to go back to the U.S. With a teary farewell, she boarded the bus for the airport in Hell after her two-week visit. She promised to come back in four months with my dad.

That night, Eilif cried, and we couldn't calm him. We rocked him, fed him, and tried every trick in our baby books. Eilif cried all night. We were now entering what the Norwegians call the *mørketid*, the dark time.

Just as daylight lasted around the clock in the summer, the sun hid behind the hills in the winter. As the winter solstice approached, the sky lightened at around 10:30 in the morning and darkened by 2:30 p.m. The Norwegian equivalent of the Minnesota north-woods motto "It's not the cold, it's the windchill" would be "It's not the cold, it's the dark." On further thought, it was also the ice. We slipped with every step . . . and the blowing hail stung each time it hit and filled my ears with little chunks of ice . . . and the rain soaked through our clothes until our nerves tingled with cold.

Just like back home in Minnesota, however, not letting the winter bother you was a sign of strength. Complaining was not an option. It was mass delusion that the cold was really not that bad. For newcomers to Norway, this was no easy task, especially with a large hill blocking our southern exposure. Our friends Knut and Inger lived on the other side of the hill, so I asked Inger if she'd seen the sun in the past weeks. "I think I saw it shine through between a couple of buildings, but there were so many clouds," she replied. "You just need to be patient for spring. The light will come back soon," she added, as though reassuring herself as well.

I asked her husband, Knut, if people in Norway got a little crazy when they were out in the middle of nowhere in the dark of winter. I told him that in the U.S., we sometimes had shootings because of people struck with cabin fever in the winter. "We're not as gun crazy as you Americans even though we have many hunting rifles," Knut said.

"You don't have all those murders that we have in the U.S.?" I asked him.

"No, in Norway we're more introverted." Knut continued, "Instead of shooting each other, we just shoot ourselves."

I checked to see if this myth of Scandinavian suicide rates was truth or fiction. It turned out that Norway had only a few more suicides per capita than the United States. I took this as consolation that the *mørketid* wouldn't be so deadly. Still, the euphoria of summer's midnight sun had disappeared, and now we had to accept the darkness.

A Muslim woman in one of my classes said that she liked the *mørketid*, although she found the shifting hours of daylight to be confusing. For example, during Ramadan she was forbidden to eat from sunup to sundown. "It's almost always dark here, so I can eat whenever I want," she said. I didn't dare mention that in several years Ramadan will come during the summer, when it never gets dark.

I told Katy that I wanted to witness the complete darkness of the *mørketid* by traveling a few hours north of Trondheim. If we were going to spend winter this far north, why didn't we plunge into it? I began planning a visit to Drægni relatives in the town of Bodø north of the Arctic Circle. I tried to convince Katy what fun we'd have. "Just think, we'll be at the same latitude as northern Alaska! We'll have the true northern Norway experience."

Katy nixed the idea. "Why don't we just turn off the lights in our apartment or lock ourselves in the closet for the same effect?"

Overhearing our conversation, a Norwegian man we had met in our birthing class tried in vain to convince us to go. "It's the best up there! I lived in Hammerfest, the northernmost city in the world, but usually spent my winters in the south," which for him meant Trondheim. Hammerfest is at 71° latitude, farther north than all of Alaska; Minneapolis, on the other hand, is at the same latitude as Milan, Italy. "I wanted to experience the darkness up there, so one winter, I stayed up there to go to school. The aurora borealis was great, but the sun never came up for a long time."

"What did you do?" I asked.

"Oh, we slept a lot. You know, like bears do in the winter. Hibernate."

Compared to Hammerfest, Trondheim's four hours of daylight was a luxury. Once the sky got dark around 2 p.m., the streetlights came on. I thought the whole town would go into semi-hibernation. Instead, the city created a cozy glow with candles burning in almost every house—especially in the windows. Businesses set the mood with candles as employees shuffled stacks of papers into file cabinets. Every night seemed to be a vigil. More candles are burned in Norway per capita—fifty-seven per person per year—than anywhere in the world. These 250 million candles burned annually in Norway are what keep the fire trucks wailing through town late at night.

As a substitute for the sun, Katy began lighting candles throughout our apartment. Still, we wanted to sleep twelve hours a day. I worried that we were going to go to bed some night and never know when to wake up because it wouldn't be light out. Maybe we'd end up hibernating until spring by accident. But our wish to sleep until it was light again in the spring was interrupted by Eilif's crying. His days and nights were mixed up because he rarely saw the light, except for glaring lightbulbs and flickering candles. He only slept a couple of hours at night, so Katy and I took turns cradling him in our arms. Actually, "cradling" was the wrong word. Eilif wouldn't calm down unless we rhythmically patted his back firmly, rocked him wildly to and fro in our arms, and actively hopped from foot to foot as though practicing the mambo. Only after I'd done this dance for a couple of hours would he calm down. I had envisioned plumping up by ten pounds over the winter, but soon realized that I was losing weight with these all-night aerobics.

We burped the baby and hoped that a bit of air was causing the discomfort. Rather than releasing a cute little puff of air, Eilif belched like a sailor and spewed a stream of spit-up down our backs. Splashes hit the floor, and we tried not to slip or let our socks absorb the liquid. Our floor turned a strange whitish hue as Eilif turned the cement into a canvas of Jackson Pollack spit-up.

I bounced Eilif for an hour. I jumped up and down and wiggled him back and forth in my arms to keep him quiet. Eilif stared transfixed at one of the Edvard Munch posters on our wall. The vivid swirls around *Madonna* kept his gaze, or maybe he just got hungry looking at those exposed breasts. I looked at Munch's other pained expressionist painting on our wall, *The Kiss,* and remembered how we got into this situation in the first place. I was thankful we had never tacked up a copy of the torturous *Scream.*

Katy woke to breast-feed Eilif some more, but he still wasn't satisfied. I took him back into the living room to calm him. Amid his incessant screaming, I sympathized with parents who shake their babies. I couldn't calm Eilif with any dance moves. I just sat down and cried along with him.

At 4 a.m., I stepped out on our third-story balcony. I felt wobbly as I stepped onto the icy snow. The cold air shocked me awake but didn't faze Eilif, bundled up in his blanket.

Suddenly, he was quiet. I looked down to see him staring wide-eyed at the green and red aurora borealis painted across the sky. The lights danced in waves directly overhead as though giant tinted spotlights were stationed at the North Pole. For once, Eilif was pleased. He was enraptured by the show and began humming softly with a slight smile on his face.

I could relax and stopped rocking Eilif, but I became anxious about the baby. Although he was wide-eyed, I couldn't see the whites of his eyes, only the pupil and dark retina. It was as though the baby were communing with his people from outer space, calling them to pick him up. Where did he come from? Who was this little creature I was holding?

I shook my head and went inside. A bit later, I looked at my watch: It was 5:30 a.m. I brought Eilif in from the balcony, and he slept a couple of hours until Katy woke up.

The only way we could get Eilif to take a nap during the day was by pushing him in his stroller into town and back. We aimed toward the bumpy cobblestones of the old town of Trondheim. Eilif needed to be vigorously bounced with his body actually springing up an inch or so from the little mattress of the stroller. The smooth cement sidewalks downtown woke him up, and he cried for more motion, more cobblestones. We were forced to lift and bounce the stroller, and Norwegians eyed us suspiciously as if we were torturing our baby. As we banged the stroller up and down, Eilif dropped back into his catnap with a little smile on his face.

We stopped in our bank where our landlord, Arne, worked. He wanted to take a good look at the new baby, so he brought us into an empty conference room. Arne lifted Eilif from the stroller—after we worked so hard to get him to sleep—and set him gently on the huge wooden table. Eilif woke and cooed and smiled at the attention. "He's very nice. You have a beautiful boy," Arne told us in English, and we smiled proudly. After a minute, Eilif shrieked, and the screams bounced around the hollow room. "This is all good. He needs to work his lungs to get strong," Arne said between the cries. "I worry when a baby is too quiet." We wrapped the baby back up and swaddled him in the stroller. Arne walked us out through the bank lobby with everyone staring at us. Arne just nodded that he was very pleased that Eilif was exercising his lungs.

Once a week, we brought Eilif to be weighed and checked out at the *helsestasjon* at the Lademoen school. All the cures that relatives had suggested had failed, so we'd asked to see the doctor about Eilif to see if he could help with the colic and reflux.

The doctor, Arvid, unwrapped Eilif, and the baby giggled with delight. "He looks perfectly happy to me," he said. Katy and I felt betrayed: Eilif was now behaving like an angel, but we knew as soon as we left the *helsestasjon* he'd fall apart. We looked like liars and crybabies.

The doctor did believe us that he cried a lot, but assured us that this would pass soon—maybe a week, maybe months. "There is nothing to do. Such is life."

We grilled Arvid about other remedies we'd heard of.

"What about chamomile?"

"*Nei,*" he responded shaking his head.

"Fennel?"

"*Nei, nei.*"

"A chiropractor?

"*Nei!*"

"Massage?"

"*Nei, nei, nei!* None of this will cure the colic," Arvid scoffed and waved his hand dismissingly at these quack remedies, as though telling us that we had to toughen up.

We looked at him silently in desperation. He broke the quiet by asking, "So the problem here is that you are tired, correct?"

Yes, we nodded.

"Then we must send the baby to the hospital so you can rest."

Katy and I looked at each other confused about this solution. "Umm, we don't feel too comfortable about being separated from the baby," she said.

"Then all three of you must go to the hospital to rest," the doctor responded.

I told Arvid that I'd heard the hospitals were too full and they'd started having people sleep in the corridors with curtains separating them. Would they roll terminally ill patients into the hall just so we could sleep for a couple of days?

The doctor shook his head. "*Nei, nei, nei*. It's OK." He assured us that there was space. "There they can do some tests on the baby while you sleep."

"But you said the baby was perfectly healthy!" Katy responded.

"Oh, he is, but if you want, they can do some tests. So what will it be, do you all want to go to the hospital until you are rested?"

It was as though the doctor was advertising the hospital as a sort of hotel for new families where they served three meals a day and took care of the baby. What a great system to help distraught parents. I thought that we were a little low on food at home and a break would be nice. Just getting a bit of rest, though, was a temporary solution, and who really wanted to stay in a hospital?

"No, really, that's OK. We can manage at home," Katy told Arvid, and I grudgingly agreed. The doctor shrugged, as though he'd offered a solution and we'd refused. Suddenly, we'd lost any right to complain.

Then the doctor held up Eilif to take another look. In a sweet voice, he asked him, "OK, you little bastard, what's your problem?"

Katy and I looked at each other in disbelief. Did he really just call our son a bastard? How could he say that? I realized that Arvid has a British accent, so he had learned his English in England where "bastard" perhaps wasn't so bad, but still . . .

"So your stomach hurts, does it, you little bastard?" he said as he gently put the stethoscope on Eilif's heart and rubbed his belly.

The doctor called Eilif a little bastard a few more times before finishing. We finally brought our baby into the waiting room and bundled him up before going back outside. A few other Norwegian mothers were cradling their calm swaddled babies in the waiting room. Katy looked longingly at these quiet infants sleeping snuggly in their arms.

Eilif startled Katy from her reverie with his piercing cry. The other mothers were shocked at the volume of his scream and looked at me as if I had pinched him. The mothers covered the ears of their babies, but it was too late. Eilif had set off a chain reaction, and the other babies began whimpering at all the noise. I put in my earplugs so I could get Eilif dressed. I couldn't help but feel a little pleased that he had shaken up things in this quiet room.

The doctor and Aslaug, the nurse, came into the waiting room to see what the problem was. We just waved proudly as we loaded Eilif into his stroller. The doctor shook his head and said, "Oh, that little bastard."

I found myself strangely proud of Eilif. I viewed him not as a fragile babe but more like Mao Zedong. I feared and admired him and would do anything for him. He could shake up a room with a single yelp. He demanded immediate service and got it. We carried his picture around with us everywhere and mounted it on our wall in a handsome frame. We didn't want people to acknowledge us but to admire the baby. We would defend him to the death. Even if we wanted to criticize our baby, we didn't dare out of fear that others would suspect that our love was insincere. Would they report us? When he did the slightest thing, we cheered. We dunked him into the warm swimming pool and cheered just as millions did when Mao swam in the Yangtze River.

To Katy, I pointed out these obvious parallels, right down to the fact that, like Mao, Eilif's head was huge in proportion to his body. Katy was not amused by my observations or my other theory that Eilif might be an alien. "Shhhh!" she told me, as though Eilif might hear and wreak his wrath upon us.

"Maybe you do need some rest in the hospital," she said.

After the appointment to find a cure for colic, we met our friend Inger at a café in town to tell her about this doctor with the awful bedside manner. Inger told us that her doctor prescribed her the wrong medicine twice for a rather serious breast infection. She still hadn't gotten the right prescription. "The doctor is going to call soon," she sighed.

I told her that in the U.S., we'd consider taping the phone conversation and suing the doctor.

She shook her head, "You're in Norway now; these things happen. Doctors are human too."

Katy didn't understand how Inger could be so calm and said, "I'd be so mad!"

"Oh, it's OK," Inger said. "In Norway, we don't try to solve these matters in the courts. There are easier solutions for everyone."

Now that we were new parents, our solution for getting inspiration and energy during the *mørketid* was switching from one vice to the next: pastries, marzipan, dark chocolate, darker coffee. Scandinavians drink more coffee per person than any other people in the world.

Chocolate is the required staple to survive a Norwegian winter. Hot cocoa filled metal thermoses, and my favorite name for a chocolate bar was called *kvikk lunsj* (quick lunch). The label of Oslo-based Freia Chocolate told how explorer Roald Amundsen thanked Freia for saving him on his trip to the South Pole. "Freia chocolate made up one of our chief food products on the voyage, and I find it to be a brilliant product," Amundsen wrote. The label of Freia *selskap sjokolade* went a step further: "In the desert of ice at the south pole, man can barely take with him everything he needs to survive. Amundsen took Freia chocolate . . . Besides being tasty nourishment, a daily ration of chocolate was an important treat to keep up their will and optimism under the most extreme circumstances." In other words, Freia chocolate not only keeps you happy, but it helped discover the South Pole. We took this to heart and dutifully ate our daily ration.

Complaining about the *mørketid* was futile since it was always darker farther north, just as it was always colder up in the mountains in Røros. Under the pinkish sunlight at midday, we wandered through the slippery cobblestone streets of the nearby Bakklandet neighborhood among the tilted wooden buildings painted every classic color approved by the Scandinavian Colour Institute. Eilif's stroller bounced in rhythm according to the cracks between the bricks underfoot.

"It now makes total sense to me why people become alcoholics in the winter here," Katy said. "And I have never craved cigarettes so much." To prevent more addicts, the Norwegian government wisely taxes alcohol and cigarettes to the point of being prohibitively expensive. That didn't stop us from occasional bottles of red wine, which we justified by saying that it was good for our hearts.

Cabin fever struck after the holidays in both Norway and its colony, Minnesota. *"Det finnes ikke dårlig vær bare dårlige klær,"* a Norwegian friend told us and then translated it as "There's no bad weather, only bad clothes." This Norwegian saying urged everyone to go outside—in proper attire—no matter what the conditions and prevent this mental illness of being cooped up. Your body could recover from a cold, but you had to work to recover from cabin fever.

In Trondheim, the biggest obstacle wasn't the cold (the lowest temperature we saw was 10 degrees), but the rain and subsequent ice. A man from Trondheim named Egil told us, "No one shovels the walk in front of their house. We like things to be like the old days. We never have shoveled the sidewalk, so why should we start now? In America, you would probably have a court case against you!"

This philosophy caused Katy and me to slip all over, even with nonslip rubber soles on our shoes. Holding on to Eilif's carriage was the only thing that prevented us from tumbling on our long trips downtown to the fish shop.

While we were walking down a big hill into the Bakklandet neighborhood, I started sliding in slow motion. I was holding onto the handle of the stroller for balance, but my feet wouldn't stop moving in tandem with the wheels. I reached to Katy to help stop me, but she was sliding too. She grasped for the stroller to keep Eilif safe, but her lack of traction sped up the stroller.

We both clung to the handle of the stroller but kept slipping. As though surfing, we stayed standing and gained speed for about thirty feet. Katy screamed that we were sliding into a busy street. Cars flicked their headlights at us when they saw us doing this slow-motion slide on the ice, but we kept going helplessly into the street. A spot of sand brought my feet to a stop in the middle of the road as cars screeched to a stop. Katy and I sighed and pushed the buggy off the road. Eilif looked up at us happily as though he wanted another ride.

Luckily most cars had spiked tires to prevent skidding on the ice and hitting tumbling pedestrians. The safest place to walk was downtown Trondheim, where most of the sidewalks were heated to melt the ice. Since Katy and I couldn't afford a car, not to mention spiked tires, we needed a way to get to town without breaking our necks. We saw an elderly woman cruising around at ten to fifteen miles per hour on a *spark,* a sort of kick sled like those used for dogsledding, except feet are used for propulsion rather than dogs. A *spark* would work fine on ice and light snow, but we wouldn't be able to go uphill or use it downtown on the heated sidewalks.

Inger told us that we need *brodder,* or spikes on our shoes, to keep from slipping. I asked some Norwegian classmates where I could find them. "Only old people wear the spikes on their shoes!" one student teased. "The main reason old people go to hospital in Norway is because they've broken their pelvis." She laughed at the idea that I would wear these spikes, but then her friend admitted that she'd had some awful falls.

"I should buy spikes, but they're terribly unfashionable," her friend said.

I found some iron cleat crampons like those used for climbing glaciers that the storekeeper insisted were for walking on the sidewalks. I wrapped the leather straps over my shoes to secure the metal spikes on my soles, so I could nearly walk up a wall of ice. When I went to class, I found myself gloating amid the disparaging looks from other students who were slipping dangerously on the sidewalk. Maybe I was breaking the rules of *Janteloven* by showing off that I was wiser than others, or maybe I was just showing that the winter was getting to me, because I'd given up any sense of style. In either case, I was beating cabin fever by getting outside.

Katy gave a pair of spikes to Inger, who had just had her baby as well. She thanked Katy for the gift and thought the spikes were great for traction. Strangely, we never saw her wear them.

I soon understood the aversion to wearing crampons when walking on the heated sidewalks of the city. My spikes on exposed cement caused occasional sparks underfoot, and I sounded like I was tap dancing. I entered a building, and the doormats stuck to my shoes, becoming welcome-mat flippers. The Norwegians inside politely looked away as I wrestled the mats from my feet.

The advantage of wearing spikes was that Katy and I could climb to the top of the hill in Trondheim. Between noon and one p.m., we got a peek at the sun poking up above the horizon. Eilif squinted the first time he saw the sun and cried. We let him cry as the sun filled our eyes and we hoped for lighter days.

Tran!

Being healthy and robust is a national obsession in Norway. Our nurse, Aslaug, at the health station met with us once a week to make sure everything was going fine and to see if we had any questions about our son, Eilif. One of her biggest concerns, however, had been that he get enough *tran,* or cod liver oil. "You must start at four weeks old and give him *tran* in every month with the letter 'R.' First you start with a few drops on your finger that you put in his mouth. He will spit it out. If you do this every day, he will spit it out. But soon he will take two and a half teaspoons of *tran* and be a healthy baby."

I asked my Norwegian teacher, Sissel, if it is normal to give babies *tran.* "Oh yes, everyone should take *tran.* I take *tran* every day because I'm very worried about getting sick," she said. "None of the other teachers ever miss a day, and you are sort of expected to come in even if you're sick. I've started taking four spoonfuls a day, even though you are only supposed to take one."

After she told me this, she came to class and had almost lost her voice. That day we had a special reading in the book about the wonders of cod liver oil, perhaps sponsored by the fish industry. Sissel advised the whole class, "You should really take some *tran* every day, and you won't get sick."

"Lofot Tran" came in a beautiful blue glass bottle with a photo of a lone fishing boat sailing by a remote Lofoten island on the label. Katy thought I was crazy to take it, but I wanted to survive the winter.

I poured one small teaspoon of Lofoten *tran* into one of the special silver spoons that Wes had given us and gulped it down. How could anything taste so horrible? One spoonful of cod liver oil is like swallowing an entire rotten fish. It slithered down my throat, and I burped up that taste all morning.

"I suppose I get some of those burps too. You get used to it," Sissel told me the next day. I had newfound respect for her four spoonfuls a day.

"During the summer school class," she said, "I talked so much about the wonders of *tran* that at the end of the session, they brought me a bottle of *tran*. I drank half of it in front of them."

I kept taking my daily *tran* but refused to have the first thing that Eilif tasted besides breast milk be cod liver oil. Aslaug, the nurse, insisted, however, explaining that babies need vitamin D because of the *mørketid*.

At the store, we found special *barnetran*, baby cod liver oil, that smelled like super-sweet syrupy candy. Eilif hated it. He wouldn't open his mouth, so we'd wait until he cried. Quickly, we'd sneak a spoonful into his mouth, and then he'd shriek for fifteen minutes. Through the fish oil, the screams sounded more like a gurgle. In any case, most of the *tran* ended up on his bib and all over his clothes. Even after the two-hour wash cycle, an odor of cod could be detected.

Katy became convinced of the curative powers of *tran* and took lemon-flavored fish oil. We then had three kinds of cod liver oil in the house, and Katy wanted to import it to the U.S.

To avoid the cod liver oil soaking into all his clothes, we fed Eilif his *tran* naked right before his bath. The oil was supposed to wash off in the tub, but it just rose to the surface and coated his skin evenly when he got out of the water.

To avoid a whole household smelling like *tran*, I took double doses to get rid of it. I mentioned that it would be great when the sun shone again, the fear of rickets subsided, and Eilif could forgo his daily *tran* soakings. Katy replied, "I think that after all the effort of getting him to take his *tran*, we should keep giving it to him."

"A lot of babies really like it," Sissel assured me.

"It makes them very smart," added Inger. I asked, how do they know *tran* makes intelligent babies? "I suppose they don't really, but who would dare risk it?"

Rakfisk: Riskier Than Lutefisk

The elementary school teachers stumbled down the steep steps, sloshing a glass of Dahl's pilsner in one hand and a shot of aquavit in the other. We'd happened upon a Norwegian Christmas tradition: the *julebord*. At these yuletide parties, anything goes. Lots of food and drink lead to workplace gossip, wild dancing, and dicey practical jokes. For instance, my Norwegian teacher's husband had his chair pulled out from under him by a drunk employee, who thought it was very funny. Her husband was laid up in bed for five weeks afterwards. In another *julebord* incident, an inebriated worker snipped off his boss's ponytail with a scissors. The worker was fired, but the union defended him, claiming that the *julebord* was somehow a valid excuse for this kind of "merriment."

Katy's dad and stepmom were visiting to see our new baby and offered to take us out for a Norwegian feast. To impress my visiting in-laws, I showed them the *Tavern på Sverresborg,* a creaky wooden tavern from 1739 turned into a Norwegian restaurant in the hills above Trondheim. A rowdy *julebord* for high school teachers celebrating the end of the semester was in full swing upstairs.

While waiting for our glasses of mulled wine, we watched one teacher nearly slide down the wooden steps from the party upstairs. Incredibly, he held his glass of beer and a shot glass perfectly steady as his feet hit the ground with a thud. He sipped his aquavit nonchalantly; here was a *julebord* pro. "This place used to be a whorehouse, you know," he spat out in perfect English (with a slight slur) as he made himself comfortable at our table. "They moved it up from the center of Trondheim. How do you do? My name is Øyvind."

Some of his colleagues smoked outside and consoled one of the teachers in a bright pink party dress who had broken down in tears in the courtyard. She wiped her running mascara on her sleeve, and soon her pink dress had zebra stripes. Our new friend Øyvind shrugged off his crying colleague, explaining that either a school romance had been uncovered or someone had played a *julebord* joke on her. He then took it upon himself to lead us through the restaurant's limited menu of *lutefisk,* reindeer heart, pancakes, a *julebuffet,* and *rakfisk.* He insisted I order the *rakfisk* with the ominous advice: "Trust me."

The waitress took the order with a suspicious grin, then Øyvind explained my fate between sips of beer. "The fishermen would take a trout, smother it in salt and sugar, and bury it underground for three to four months. As soon as the whole town stunk like rotting fish, the hungry villagers would simply follow their noses to the hidden treasures. You must be careful not to touch the fish, or the bacteria from your hands can infect it."

"And the dirt isn't full of bacteria?" I asked.

"Just last week, five people up in Nord-Trøndelag had to go to hospital because they made their own *rakfisk.* Do you say 'botulism' in English?" I remembered that *rakfisk* was the "fermented fish" that the midwife Sigrid had warned us about.

Øyvind explained that his mother had made some *rakfisk* last week for their Christmas party next week. "She tried it out the day before. She called us every few hours to tell us she was OK. You usually feel the effects of bad *rakfisk* within about five hours when your hands go numb. Then you must call the hospital as soon as possible. It's a very risky sport to eat this food!"

Øyvind excused himself to get another beer just as the waitress set down a plate of cold, neon-orange fish that carried a distinct smell of petroleum. I asked her, "This is the *rakfisk*? And it's safe?" She laughed and walked back to the kitchen without answering. I saw Øyvind out in the courtyard smoking and telling a funny story to the colleague who was crying earlier. Was he describing how he convinced these gullible Americans to eat rotten fish? Could this be a *julebord* practical joke that would give us food poisoning all in good fun?

I pierced the soft fish with my fork and sliced a chunk. Neither Katy nor her parents dared risk the *rakfisk* and ordered pancakes or the Christmas buffet. They stared as I lifted the morsel of orange fish smothered in sour cream and onions to my mouth. With Øyvind's words "Trust me" ringing through my head, I chewed the succulent fish. The salty meat melted away in my mouth, and I was surprised at how good I found it. "Mmmm!" I said. "It's delicious. Would anyone like to try some?"

I finished the whole plate of *rakfisk* with relish, but my stomach started to gurgle. I needed water, lots of water. When that didn't quench my thirst, I drank beer. Øyvind came in from the courtyard to rescue me by insisting that I guzzle a bit of eighty-proof aquavit. "It's the water of life! You really need to have it with the *rakfisk* because it makes it much more edible and could even kill the bacteria if it's gone bad."

My stomach stopped churning, or perhaps my senses were just numb from the liquor. I'd been trying to be on good behavior for my in-laws, but my speech slurred. Øyvind smiled as he watched the aquavit take effect. In spite of my slowed responses, I knew I was the victim of a *julebord* prank of getting drunk in front of my wife's parents. I couldn't do a thing about it as I tried to focus on Øyvind through my blurry vision and could only sip more aquavit to suppress the dangerous dinner.

Juletid

"Christmas is the antidote to the darkness," a Norwegian friend told me, and food and drink are the ingredients of Christmas. By November, *Juletid* (Yuletide) preparations were in full swing; however, many Norwegians succumbed to the temptation of cheap charter flights to the Canary Islands, Madeira, and Majorca and the promise of free-flowing Sangria, but I'm sure these snowbirds grew nostalgic for a white Norwegian Christmas.

Our local Rimi supermarket was full of Christmas products, which were the same as what they sold all year round but with the word *Jul* written across the packaging in red and green letters. Even though the average Norwegian consumes 150 liters of milk per year, the dairy industry pushed its *julemelk* (Christmas milk) with decorative packaging to match the supper table. Next to the dairy case stood precarious stacks of *julebrus* (Christmas pop) and even Christmas toilet paper with little drawings of Santa Claus. I wanted to buy a *julemarzipangris* (Christmas marzipan pig), but the Rimi shopkeeper Eirik warned me, "You can't buy the marzipan pig; you must win it."

The Vinmonopolet was pushing its *Juleakevitt*, Christmas aquavit, and a magazine article described the forty different kinds of aquavit that were perfect for the holidays, including "Lutefisk Akevitt" and "Rakfisk Akevitt." Our teacher Solveig told us that because of the high cost ($14 for a small shot of akevitt at the *Tavern på Sverresborg*), "my father used to make moonshine at home, and we always had to draw the curtains and say that he was 'baking.'"

The main culinary attraction, however, was the *julepølse* (Christmas wieners), which looked just the same as the regular disgusting hot dogs sold year-round. Our Norwegian friend

Rachel was dumbfounded when she heard I didn't like hot dogs. "What do you mean? They're so much better than American hot dogs. Some of the best *pølser* are the ones made from hamburger meat that is shaped like a *pølse,* I suppose because then they don't put in all those strange pork parts."

Rachel didn't like them wrapped in a *lompe,* or lefse, but preferred the regular white hot dog bun. "The best *pølse* are the ones with bacon wrapped around them. Those are my favorite! They have cheese inside of them too. They're delicious!"

I told her husband, Arild, that we didn't eat wieners for Christmas but my dad convinced us to make lefse. We made stacks of the tortilla-like potato delicacies and filled them with cinnamon or raspberry jam.

"You actually make lefse?" Arild said. "We never do that here. We just buy it in the store." At the Rimi supermarket, special packages of *julelefse* were on sale.

For our first Christmas with a baby, I wanted to do something memorable. In the old mining town of Røros up in the snowy hills toward Sweden, you can herd reindeer in the wintertime. I called up the organization for more information. I told the receptionist in Røros that I'd like to bring my family to see the reindeer. "They're really beautiful animals," I said.

"Yes," she replied, "we like to eat them."

Going into the woods to slaughter a reindeer for Christmas dinner wasn't the kind of tradition I wanted to start for our new family. When I told this to my Italian classmate Juri, he couldn't understand why I thought this was so wrong. "I very much want to know how to cook a reindeer," he replied. "This is something which I cannot find in Genova, so I want to eat one while I'm here."

Even our jolly landlord, Arne, didn't see the reindeer as a protected Christmas symbol. His wife, Oddbjørg, told us their family's Christmas tradition, "Arne dresses like Santa Claus; then we go eat reindeer."

"Reindeer? You actually eat Santa's reindeer?" Katy asked.

Arne rubbed his belly and said, "Yes, they are very good."

Meanwhile, the Norwegian version of Santa Claus, the *jule-nissen,* just gets gruel. A bowl of porridge is left out in the barn for the Christmas elf. Farmers who forget will suffer a year of bad luck for not feeding the *nisse.*

When I spoke about the elves in the barn, Knut corrected me. "*Nisse* are pixies, which are very different from elves, gnomes, or trolls. If you don't treat your animals right, you will have problems with the pixies because they look after the animals." Knut explained that trolls usually have multiple heads and are cruel but very stupid. *Nisse,* on the other hand, are kind as long as you are good as well. An article in the newspaper even told how a farmer refused orders by the municipality to tear down a decrepit old barn because he feared the wrath of the *nisse.* This must be why Norway has no factory farms.

I told Knut about the town in northern Finland that has Santa Claus's house, so tourists fly in from around the world. "Finland? No, no, no. Santa Claus lives in Norway," he insisted. Apparently, Santa Claus lives in every barn with the animals.

When Katy and I went shopping in downtown Trondheim a few days before Christmas, dozens of Santa Clauses holding hands extended from the grocery store across one of the bridges all the way into town. They were trying to set the world record for the largest chain of *julenisser.*

Meanwhile just outside of a grocery store was a procession of Santa Lucia with girls dressed in white robes carrying saffron-colored buns and wearing a crown of lingonberry greens with lit candles to keep away the darkness. This pageant with carolers singing the Neapolitan folk song of Santa Lucia was more of an imported Christmas tradition from Sweden. Most Norwegian families don't celebrate Santa Lucia Day; perhaps the free upbringing for children doesn't condone Black Peter, who carries coal to the disobedient children.

With holiday activities in full swing, Katy and I followed Inger's advice and bought some *ribbe,* pork ribs, to have a traditional Norwegian Christmas Eve dinner. As I prepared the ribs on Christmas Eve, I looked out the kitchen window to the graveyard across the street. Hundreds of candles lit the cemetery with a peaceful glow during this darkest time of the year. Just like on All Saints' Day, many Norwegian families braved the cold to sit in the cemetery for hours to be with the departed souls of their loved ones.

To keep the chill out, Katy stoked the stove with wood from the enormous log pile in the living room. We felt like we were in a cabin or a barn rather than a bland three-story apartment building.

We had dragged a giant Christmas tree up the flights of stairs to fill our living room and bent the tip of the towering pine to squeeze it into the apartment. Once the tree was up, Katy and I remembered that we had no decorations. We explained our situation to Inger when she called to wish us a merry Christmas. She recognized this as an emergency and came right over.

While eating spicy ginger cookies and drinking strong *gløgg* (warm spiced wine), we learned from Inger how to make Norwegian heart-shaped ornaments to hang on our tree. She explained how today little children go caroling door-to-door dressed as *julenisser,* Christmas pixies, with a little sack to get treats. No kids bothered climbing three flights of steps to sing in our apartment. Instead we followed another Norwegian Christmas tradition and sang carols around the newly decorated Christmas tree.

As Inger prepared to go home, we confessed to her that the lack of sun in this darkest week of the year was wearing us down.

"Spring will be here soon," Inger reassured us.

"Oh really, like February?" I asked hopefully.

"Or in March, like Minnesota?" added Katy.

"Well, what is 'spring'?" Inger asked. "In Trondheim, we really don't have spring until late April, but even then it can snow."

As Inger was stepping out the door, the Lademoen church bells pealed loudly. Just like Cinderella, Inger said that she had to get home. Over the din, she explained that at 5 p.m. on Christmas Eve is when the bells ring to officially *"ringe in Julen"* (ring in Christmas).

According to the cookbook, the ribs were ready. I pulled out the huge slab of meat and put it on the table.

"Umm, now how do we eat it?" Katy asked.

I had no idea. We stared at the soft gooey meat and cut into the inch of fat on top. The meat was scarce and could only be retrieved thanks to the diligence of two famished people.

The phone rang. It was Inger calling to see how the ribs turned out. Katy sat on the couch holding her belly, and I was feeling queasy too. Inger said that the top fatty part is supposed to turn crispy like a pork rind or bacon and peel off. Perhaps out of pity, Inger and Knut invited us over on Christmas Day to eat lutefisk. The thought of fish soaked in drain cleaner wasn't particularly appealing at the moment, but we accepted nonetheless.

Rather than feel sorry for ourselves thousands of miles from home, we bundled up in front of the roaring fire next to the evergreen tree with our newborn baby.

Fish in Lye

The fishmonger at Fiskehallen had encouraged customers months before to order their *lutefisk* ahead of time so they wouldn't disappoint their guests at Christmas dinner. *Lutefisk* remains one of the most popular, if notorious, Norwegian Christmas traditions.

My father once made a *lutefisk* dinner for my family in Minnesota at Christmas. He waited in line at Ingebretsen's Scandinavian market on Lake Street in Minneapolis for a package of this preserved cod. While the deli sells 1,500 pounds of meatballs and Swedish sausage on average during the holidays, my dad opted for the mushy translucent fish in a plastic bag for our Christmas feast. He heated up the *lutefisk* in bowls, and the white fish that nearly dissolved into a Jell-O-like mess was passed around the table. We each spooned a bit of the wiggling fish mush into our bowls with a plop.

"This was a delicacy that our ancestors from the Sognefjord could only afford once a year," my dad announced. Then he added, "Oh, put a pat of butter on top to bring out the flavor." One by one we pushed the *lutefisk* away as my dad kept encouraging us to discover our Norwegian roots. He valiantly finished two spoonfuls and kept passing the *lutefisk* around encouraging us, "We wouldn't want to waste all this good fish, now, would we?" Finally, even he had to concede that it was inedible. When we served the fish to our cats, they licked the butter off the top but wouldn't touch the fish.

When I told my story to our Norwegian friend Aud, she scoffed, "Obviously, you didn't cook it right. *Lutefisk* should be firm, flaky, and not like gelatin!" I realized that I had made a deadly mistake. I should have said that I had tried *lutefisk* and enjoyed it very much, thank you. Instead, Aud insisted that while in Norway, I eat it and like it.

She explained the process for making *lutefisk:* "First you dry the cod for months; then you put it in *lut*—do you know *lut*? You can use it to take the paint off of wood. It is what you use to clean out your sink when it is stuck." So the fish tastes like drain cleaner? Aud ignored the question and continued extolling the virtues of this "lye-fish." "When you are ready to cook it, you soak the fish in water. There should be no yellow left; otherwise, it has too much *lut* left and doesn't taste so good." I asked her what other poisons have been tried by these inventive Norwegians to preserve their food. When I pressed her to answer if anyone had ever gotten sick from this questionable method of preserving food, she replied, "You Americans! You're always so obsessed with cleanliness and worried about getting sick from everything!"

Lutefisk probably dates back to the time of the Vikings. The legend goes that Viking fishermen hung the cod to dry on tall birch racks, as is still practiced today in the Lofoten Islands. Neighboring, unfriendly Vikings (probably Swedes) attacked and burned the racks of fish, but a rainstorm from the North Sea doused the fire. The dried fish soaked in this puddle of water and birch ash (essentially lye) for months. Hungry Vikings discovered the reconstituted cod and had a feast. Only after the first brave diners held their stomachs in agony did the second group of Norwegians realize that the *lutefisk* needed to be rinsed first.

The first proof of *lutefisk* in print is in the book *Nordic Cultural and Natural History* from 1555 by Olaus Magnus. "Soak dried fish two days in a strong lye solution and one day in fresh water to make fine food." The key word is *fine,* which could either mean "good" or simply "edible." How many Norwegians had died figuring out how long the fish needed to be rinsed?

Aud was pleased when I told her that our Norwegian friends Knut and Inger had invited us over to their apartment for a *lutefisk* dinner. Surprisingly, Inger had never eaten *lutefisk*; perhaps her family had revolted after being served too many herring cakes.

The day of the dinner Knut called up and asked, "Is a suit and tie OK?"

I couldn't tell if he meant for himself or me. Knut is a dapper dresser who even wears a sport coat when going to the local café, so I thought he must have been teasing me about my slovenly clothes. I thought of Christmas as a laid-back affair, but I went along with his joke and said, "Um sure, Knut. I can wear a suit."

"Great!" he responded, and I realized he wasn't kidding. "If you don't wear a tie for Christmas dinner in America, when do you get dressed up?" he asked.

When we arrived, the best porcelain, silver, and crystal were set perfectly on the table. Tall green candles burned as the centerpiece. During the course of the dinner, we were impressed that we managed to use seven different glasses — one for beer, white wine, red wine, water, aquavit, coffee, and an after-dinner drink. Inger told us not to worry about the dishes because they have a dishwasher.

Knut cooked the light and flaky cod preserved in lye to perfection. The *lutefisk*'s lack of flavor was covered up by *lutefiskbacon*, rich mashed green peas, and strong eighty-proof aquavit. Inger confessed this was the first time she'd eaten *lutefisk* and didn't particularly care for it, which was why they cooked moose steaks to fill us up. "My brother shoots a moose every year, and so we fill our freezer," Knut said. "Moose is the only red meat we eat in our house, because it's lean and tasty. You know that the beef you find in Norway are old dairy cows that don't produce milk anymore, not cattle raised just for food like in the U.S. That's why Norwegian hamburgers taste funny. You should really eat moose." The rich meat tasted like the best lean Angus beefsteak I'd ever had.

Knut and Inger wanted to show us a true Christmas dinner, so we had hand-picked cloudberries with cream. Orange cloudberries, "Norwegian gold," grow only in the mountain moors. Inger explained that "most Norwegians put an almond in the *rømmegrøt* (cream porridge) and whoever finds it gets the lucky marzipan pig. We decided to put the almond in the dessert instead." The four of us dug into the dessert, but the cloudberries had large, hard seeds that were more intense than blackberry seeds. The one almond went missing because whoever had the almond just ate it thinking it was another one of the hard seeds. Who gets the candy pig? No one at the table except for me actually liked marzipan. I was awarded the Christmas pig.

Born Wearing Skis

"All we did in the winter was homework and ski jumping," an older man from nearby Orkanger reminisced to me. "You had to build your own ski jumps. We didn't have much downhill skiing then because you had to prepare your own hills. Nowadays, all the young people have the hills prepared for them. To start ski jumping, you must go up to the Bymarka park to the different levels of ski jumps. Back then, you just went down the jumps; it was natural. Some kids were afraid, though. Maybe they didn't jump because it was always dark. Then they didn't have anything to do in the winter except for study."

I asked if he still jumped. "Well, I stopped when I broke my pelvis. Now I have an artificial hip. Most people don't hurt themselves too badly, though. They usually stop when they are about thirty years old and have a wife and child and can't risk it anymore. It's not really dangerous at all, though," he insisted as he limped away.

This passion for frozen danger seeped under the surface of Norwegian passivity, as evidenced by Trondheim's huge ski jump, which swoops down so steeply that locals couldn't bear to see it sit dormant in the summer months. During the summer, a special surface was rigged up for slippery descents and smooth landings on the grass below.

Downhill skiing is less popular, but buses run from downtown to resorts or over the border into Sweden. Further south, skiers slalom down glaciers all summer long. Alpine skiing had mostly replaced Telemark-style skiing, or downhill skiing using cross-country skis, after Norwegian students saw Norwegian Americans doing graceful Telemark turns in the Midwest.

When Norwegians talk about skiing, though, they mean

cross-country, or Nordic skiing. Monty Python spoofed Norwegians with a sketch of the people never taking off skis, even in bed. A Norwegian friend's mom was insulted and complained that "they don't understand that skis can be very useful!"

At the Lademoen school, I witnessed a group of early elementary schoolkids running around the playground during recess on short plastic skis playing soccer. How the kids could kick and not tumble over convinced me that this could be a new sport for the winter Olympics.

To make the most of the dark winter, many kilometers of cross-country ski trails were lit late into the night just on the outskirts of town in the Bymarka park. Groomed trails wound through the ancient pine tree forests and around big boulders, which were the legendary frozen trolls who were turned to stone when they saw the sun, according to Norwegian legends. The shadows from the stars and northern lights were obliterated when another overhead light popped on to mark the ski trail. The air carried the aroma of juniper berries mixed with fresh evergreens to spur on the skiers. The blanket of snow deadened the sound, but the cold, crisp air made sound waves clearer so any approaching skier could be heard a kilometer away.

In Trondheim's center, I often saw people lugging their skis and poles to hop on the bus or tram for a couple hours skiing after work. No salt or sand was used on the roads near the park, so sleds and skis ruled the roads. An older woman zoomed across the snow on a wooden *spark*. Groceries or a child could sit on the front of the *spark* while the adult stood on the long metal runners and pushed with a kick.

Katy and I stuck to cross-country skiing and went to a resort near Lillehammer for a weekend. The hotel served gourmet breakfast and dinner buffets and afternoon heart-shaped waffles with strawberries and *rømme* sour cream.

The other skiers at this resort in Gausdal made themselves

very comfortable indeed. Perhaps the fresh mountain air let everyone relax and forget the pretensions of the city. We saw uninhibited guests getting dressed in the hallway and others who left their doors and curtains wide open at all times. One man went regularly to meals dressed in long underwear, and the hotel resorted to calling for a "formal dinner" to get him and others to dress up.

We didn't come to the mountains to be pampered, though; we came for excitement and danger. A flyer in the hotel advertised for the summer "Bicyclists for Birkebeiner," in which they'd ride mountain bikes straight down the treacherous ski runs to see who could make it to the bottom in one piece. Another poster advertised the Postal Museum in Lillehammer that showed how a brave postman dug himself out of an avalanche with his mail horn.

With these models of valor, Katy and I prepared for our cross-country skiing adventure in the Norwegian mountains. Rather than leaving our newborn Eilif with a babysitter, Norwegian friends insisted that our tiny four-month-old go along with us. "He was born in Norway, right? Then the fresh air will do him good. Babies shouldn't stay at home but should go out. You know what we say, 'Norwegian babies are born with skis on, the parents provide the poles.'"

The woman at the ski rental shop fixed us up with a *pulk*, a sled for babies with plenty of straps to assure he won't slide out. On a map, she pointed out the easiest path, which passes an old lodge. "You can get waffles and hot wine there. With that route, you pass it twice!"

She glanced at the giant Swix thermometer outside to choose the appropriate color of wax or klister for the day. "It's best to get the ski wax from the area it's made. Swix works the best in Norway because it's from here," she advised us.

Mostly, I was worried about irritated moose crossing our path, after hearing that a sixty-eight-year-old man had a near-fatal experience in Gausdal with a wounded moose he shot.

The 650-pound animal appeared dead until he approached. The moose sprang to its feet when the man touched it and thrashed about. The man held on to its rack to avoid being skewered for the last couple minutes of the animal's life.

The women at the rental shop told me not to worry about the "King of the Forest," the moose, and told us about the drunken moose alert near Telemark. The cold snap hit the apples and berries before they fell to the ground; when warm weather came back, the fruit fermented on the branches. Hungry moose gobbled up the alcoholic berries and either lay down for a nap or attacked. She said that this explained why a moose fell on a red Mazda on Highway 405 just south of Vatnestrom. The 700-pound beast then jumped into the next lane of traffic, where another car barreled into it. Fortunately, the people were only a little bruised, and the drunken moose became supper.

Somehow this wasn't reassuring as we clipped on our skis and I attached the *pulk* around my waist. The last sight before entering the forest was the Vikingland Bar, where dozens of empty beer bottles were plunked into snowdrifts along the icy path. The trail skirted along the edge of the mountains, and the sun made the fields of snow shimmer like glitter.

Norwegians stopped all along the trail to picnic on *smørbrød* with *brunost* (sandwiches with brown cheese) and were unconcerned about any unruly moose. Some picnickers assured us that moose attacks are extremely rare. Perhaps we could relax as well. Then we heard about a group of picnickers who encountered an annoyed moose during their winter vacation. Their dog ran circles around the giant animal, but when a kid threw a bun at the moose's head, the beast lost it. The picnic was over as everyone scrambled up into the trees to watch the crazed moose run in circles down below. Another skier approached unaware of the angry moose, which lowered its head and knocked him to the ground. Just when the moose was ready to trounce on the fallen man, another skier whacked the moose in the head with his skis. Incredibly, the moose regained its composure and scurried off into the woods.

The picnickers laughed at the story about the dumb moose, but we weren't interested in challenging a drunken moose with bakery goods. When we stopped for a break, I pulled out a pamphlet about winter survival I had picked up at the hotel and turned to the page about moose. A wildlife expert named Stein Strømmen was quoted as saying, "Moose will give clear warnings before they attack. First they run at you . . ."

I had heard enough. Eilif loved the cold, fresh air, which put him right to sleep in the *pulk,* but it was time to make it the four miles back to the hotel in one piece. Other skiers pulling a *pulk* didn't have nearly as much trouble as I did. Uphill was double the weight; downhill was double the speed and twice as hard to avoid trees. The "easy trails" in Norway were the same as double black diamond trails in Minnesota. The simplest trails had large hills with a quick curve at the bottom, with pines placed to catch those who couldn't turn in time.

In our rush to get back to the hotel, I took a hill too fast. As I gathered speed, the *pulk* pushed me even faster. I quickly glanced back and could see Eilif's little face sound asleep. I tried to snowplow, but my skis wouldn't leave the deep ruts. I was left with little choice but to ride out the hill. I knew I'd probably end up in a giant snowdrift, and I had no postal horn to dig myself out. I had almost arrived at the bottom of the huge hill when I noticed the sharp turn across a small bridge over a frigid creek. I bent my knees and assumed the bombing position to make a smooth turn. I was just about over the bridge when the waist strap of the *pulk* pulled me sideways. While I had dug in the side of my skis to make the turn, the *pulk* with Eilif in it was sliding right off the side of the little wooden bridge. I dug in my ski poles and pushed forward with all my might. The *pulk* skirted the lip of the bridge but made it to the other side without sliding off the edge.

I was shaking as I stopped to catch my breath. I looked into the *pulk*, worried that Eilif would be overcome by fright, but he was sleeping snugly in the sleeping bag, oblivious to the dangers around him. When we arrived back at the hotel, I was thankful to see the guy running around in his long underwear and the men on crutches telling us that ski jumping isn't dangerous at all.

"The World's Most Beautiful Voyage"

It was February, and still winter showed little sign of disappearing. We had slightly more light than during the solstice, but still we craved the sun. My parents, who had come back to visit four months after the birth, now saw that we needed a break. They offered to take us on a trip.

Every day when we walked into town, we saw the placards in front of the travel agents boasting cheap trips to the Mediterranean. Our friend Knut told us that many Norwegian businesses planned big meetings in Spain rather than in town because it was actually cheaper. Katy and I resisted the urge to just pack up for two weeks to lie in the sun. We decided that since we were in Norway, we should see as much as we could.

I suggested we take the coastal steamer up north to visit the Drægni relatives in Bodø, and my dad seconded the idea. Finally, he'd be able to meet our long-lost Norwegian relatives. Bodø is well north of the Arctic Circle and would be just coming out of complete darkness with a couple of hours of sunlight each day. I'd heard that the ancient Greek explorer Pytheas wrote about traveling to Ultima Thule (probably northern Norway) around 300 BC. Pytheas said that the days and nights in Ultima Thule lasted for six months and that the sea there was so thick (presumably with ice) the rowers could not get through it.

Katy was skeptical about a trip to the Arctic with a newborn, but travel brochures raved about "The World's Most Beautiful Voyage." The coastal steamers took eleven days to travel from Bergen up the coast of Norway, over the top to Russia, and back. Originally, the boats were the only transportation to many of the islands and remote towns of Norway, which earned the steamers the name of Hurtigruten, or the fast route. The catalog's photographs of icebergs, fjords, and reindeer changed Katy's mind.

I told the travel agent that we'd like to book four boat tickets to Bodø.

"Where? Is that in Norway?" she asked.

I was confused because it's a relatively large city. "Yes, Bodø, Norway," I said.

"I'm sorry, that's in Sweden, not Norway. There are no boats there because it's inland."

I realized my pronunciation must be a little off, so I kept trying different variations. "Buu-Doo. Boh-Da. Boo-Dah..."

"Buda, like Budapest?" she asked hopefully.

I found a map of Norway on her desk and pointed it out. "Ah! Bodø! You mean Bodø," she exclaimed.

I was certain I had pronounced it the same way, but I noticed that I lacked the emphasis. I pronounced it again, "Boo-Dah," but this time I bobbed my head forcefully with each syllable. I felt like I was mocking her, but she responded happily, "Yes, yes. That's right." Now that we were certain which city was our destination, she could book our tickets. The prices were breathtaking, but my student discount made the trip possible.

A few days later, we boarded the Hurtigruten ship, which was more of a luxury cruise ship than an old-fashioned steamer. Brass railings and marble floors made up the decor. The front lounge housed a grand piano for evening concerts, and sweeping two-story windows looked out on the snow-covered mountains that seemed to erupt from the shoreline.

My parents, Katy, and I sat in the swivel chairs enjoying the wintry view from the toasty warm inside. The motion of the boat calmed Eilif like an enormous cradle rocking him over the waves. Soon, the baby needed more motion and insisted on being pushed in his stroller outside on the deck with the fresh air, snowflakes, and wind whipping through my hair.

I met a British couple who had been on the boat since Bergen—just two days of their eleven-day trip to Russia. Already weary and slightly seasick from the trip, they told me about the Internet connection, the evening films, and other distractions from the actual boat trip that had made their time tolerable.

They led me to a PowerPoint presentation on the northern lights that was just getting started. I found my family, and we piled into the little theater. The tour director flashed dramatic photos of the aurora borealis that had been taken from the ship. R-r-r-r-ring! R-r-r-r-ring! Her cell phone rang furiously from the podium; she took the call in the middle of the show. She chatted for a few minutes to a friend as the audience watched. After a few minutes, she told the caller, "I should probably go now."

The show went on as she explained how the Japanese come on the Hurtigruten ships to venture past the Arctic Circle. They believed that seeing the midnight sun and aurora borealis promised the birth of a boy and an easy delivery. Just when she was about to reveal more myths surrounding the phenomenon, her cell phone interrupted the presentation again. R-r-r-ring! Eilif was fed up with sitting still, so Katy and I took him on another vigorous walk.

The Hurtigruten had been weaving its way between islands and the mainland, but now the captain warned that he had to navigate the ship into the open sea after the port of Rorvik. At least half of the passengers disembarked when the ship pulled into the little town. The captain advised passengers to brace for a rough ride for the next couple of hours because the North Sea was especially turbulent that day. The ship's staff passed out flattened white sacks that read *reisesykepose*, or travel sickness bag.

Katy and I ran with Eilif to our cabin in the bow of the boat and assumed that my parents were next door in theirs. The door of our cabin offered instructions in many languages of the nine steps required to put on life jackets and rain gear that completely cover the body. *Reisesykeposer* were tucked in the bookshelves and scattered amid the magazines. I assured Katy that I hadn't had motion sickness since I was a kid, so I'd at least be able to calm the baby.

The waves of the North Sea hit the boat. Katy was lying down on her bed with Eilif. I looked out the secured portal onto the sea but saw only the spray splashing against the little round window. The feeling of each wave was that of a roller coaster pushing my body up to weightlessness and then crashing down so my legs could barely hold me up. For balance, I grasped the bookshelf, which was tightly fastened to the wall like everything else in the room. Hand over hand, grabbing anything to stay on my feet, I managed to get to my bed. I plopped down hard and felt as though an invisible anvil was pushing my bones into the mattress. The bathroom door swung open and shut with a bang. Katy begged me to lock it, but if I moved I'd see my lunch again. I tried to lift myself from my new union with the mattress, but it was like doing push-ups with a Viking on my back. Katy had wisely put a bucket on the side of her bed and made use of it at regular intervals.

Eilif, on the other hand, shouted with glee. He didn't notice that his parents were incapacitated and couldn't help him. Eilif sat up on the bed and cooed with joy as each wave rocked him.

After almost two hours of rugged travel, the ship entered calm waters. Eilif was disappointed, and our legs were wobbly. We ventured out of our cabin in search of fresh air. Katy's face was pale, and our hands were clammy. My parents were calmly reading their books near the reception area.

"Hi there!" they exclaimed happily. "How are you?" We told them about our awful last hour.

"I remembered from my days in the Coast Guard that you always go to the exact middle of the ship when you hit rough seas," my dad said, and added that he couldn't find us. My dad told about one of his Coast Guard buddies who used to wear a bucket around his neck for the first couple of days at sea. Our stomachs churned.

DING! DING! DING! The dinner bell clanged and saved us from my dad's stories about the icebreaker on Lake Superior. Passengers rushed to the dining room, but Katy and I couldn't bear the thought of eating. We went back to our cabin, thankful that Eilif was now ready to sleep.

At noon the next day, we crossed the Arctic Circle. Small icebergs floated near the boat, and the sun shone just above the southern horizon. Most of the passengers gathered outside on the top deck in the crisp weather amid the fresh fallen snow. I hadn't known that they had to shovel the deck of ships in Norway.

The ship's intercom announced that all greenhorns had to pile on to the deck for the Norwegian initiation to the Arctic. One of the crew wore a ragged white beard and was dressed up in a long purple cape covered by a fishing net riddled with snagged starfish. This was Neptune, god of the sea, who had to welcome everyone who had never been this far north. Newcomers lined up as he scooped his giant ladle into a bucket of ice water and poured it down their backs.

I asked Katy if she wanted to get in line.

"Now why would I want to pour ice water down my neck and risk hypothermia? Why would I do that?"

Perhaps wanting to be accepted by the Norwegians, my dad and I stepped up to be doused with ice water. Neptune put an extra ladle full down my front just for good measure. I gasped for air as my heart seemed to stop. I ripped off my wet shirt, exposing my bare skin to the Arctic air. A member of the crew handed my dad and me a glass of wine and a certificate that we had officially passed the Arctic Circle. As the frigid winds swept across our wet bodies, my dad and I shivered violently while my mom and Katy shot a photo. We ran across the slippery deck into the sizzling sauna.

The temperature in the sauna was set at 190° Fahrenheit. The sauna had a rule of enforced nudity, and one of the sauna walls was a floor-to-ceiling window. My dad and I joined a few Norwegian men, and we watched the black-and-white landscape of rocks and snow pass by us. I wondered if the crew cleared out the saunas when we arrived at port to avoid public nudity.

The heat rose to my head as salty sweat trickled down my brow and stung my eyes. My dad wisely got out of the sauna to avoid overheating, but I held on a bit longer to prove my toughness. I felt dizzy, and the swaying of the boat reminded me of last night. A scratchy announcement over the intercom—there were even speakers in the sauna—warned that we were going to be on the open sea again and to expect some "small waves."

One of the Norwegian men threw a couple of ladles of water on the hot rocks of the sauna, and the temperature in the tiny room seemed to double. The steam pierced my pores, and I was covered in water. I stood up while I could, but the blood rushed to my head. I reached for the wooden railing but missed my first grab and clutched air. I timed my next reach with the swaying of the boat and successfully grasped the wooden handrail that protected bathers from touching the stove. The scalding wood of the railing shocked my body awake just in time to realize that the flimsy two-by-two board guarding the stove was mostly decorative.

I pushed open the door and relished the cold breeze in the locker room and the frigid water of the shower. We were finally in the Arctic.

Snowbound in Bodø

The gangplank from the Hurtigruten touched the cement pier of Bodø, and we could walk on solid ground, or at least snow. A man with dark hair and a square face who was probably sixty years old stood on the edge of the water waiting for the ferry. He could be swapped for any of my reticent uncles back home; he must be a Drægni.

"I'm sorry we don't have much snow now," Magne apologized as he greeted us. A few days ago, he said, a meter and a half covered the ground, but now barely three inches were left. He was apologetic that the weather had turned so warm and mild.

His wife, Rigmor, a woman with deep red hair, wasn't concerned about the weather. She just wanted to get her hands on the "new little Drægni Viking." Eilif felt at home as he recognized Rigmor as someone who knew how to dote on babies. As soon as we got back to their house, she asked us, "*Spiser han grøt?*" Then she translated, sort of: "Does he eat *grøt*?"

We didn't know what exactly she meant, but we'd heard stories about bizarre food eaten in northern Norway, where marrow from reindeer bones is a prized delicacy, warm "blood bouillon" with kneaded blood and fat balls is a specialty of reindeer herders, and a thick drink of seagull eggs and eighty-proof aquavit washes it all down.

We were skeptical of what she wanted to feed him since the only sustenance besides breast milk that Eilif had eaten so far was cod liver oil.

With Katy's permission, Rigmor made a bowl of *grøt*, warm porridge, for Eilif, which he ate with relish even though much of his first meal ended up across his face. Eilif grabbed the spoon from Rigmor and flicked a bit of *grøt* across the room. She just laughed at his plucky determination.

My newfound relatives chatted with my parents. My dad talked about the time we met Magne's parents, Ola and Lina, who had since passed away. Magne told us about Bodø and the ski trails that wound up into the hills. Rigmor wanted to know all about the birth. The conversation continued as everyone seemed vaguely uncomfortable. What did we have in common except for a bloodline and physical characteristics? Somehow the uneasiness didn't matter because we were all family. With relatives, you're supposed to feel a bit awkward, and there's a certain comfort in that. They're there whether you want them or not. The anxiety of meeting unknown family faded, and we formed a new bond that hadn't been there for three generations.

Of all our Drægni/Dregni relatives, Magne was the only one of his generation who was still in Norway. My dad and I are the only Dregni relatives that he had met. Now he had his wife, Rigmor, though, a voluntary bond that somehow superseded simple bloodlines. They had two grown kids: a family.

When he was young, Magne moved away from his home in western Norway and followed a job in the Arctic. I asked if he'd thought about moving back to the remote Drægni farm. He responded, "I've lived in Bodø since 1964, so why would I move back to the Lusterfjord?"

To me, it seemed obvious that everyone wants to find his or her roots and stay there, but I realized I just wanted some relatives to always be back at the original house and for it to remain unchanged for generations. I couldn't understand that if Magne knew his roots, why would he want to give them up and move to the whiter pastures of the Arctic? Perhaps because my impoverished branch of the family had left more than a century ago, I had a bucolic vision that somehow we could all reunite in the Lusterfjord now that Norway wasn't so poor. Somehow this would do my great-grandfather justice.

Magne stood at the picture window of the living room and pointed proudly across the fjord. On the other side of the bay is the Saltstraumen maelstrom, where many sailors have lost their lives. Their bodies were rarely recovered, as they were forced to the bottom of the strait by the swirling whirlpool.

A bridge spans the sixteen-yard stretch of water where 480 million cubic yards of water pass through twice a day. The high and low tides form a dangerous vortex that has swallowed boats in the mad rush of water. Seagulls circled overhead waiting for doomed fish that had been sucked into the maelstrom. Even though the Hurtigruten boat stays clear of this dangerous water flow, I breathed a sigh of relief that we would take the train back to Trondheim.

After a big lunch of smoked salmon on scrambled eggs, Magne drove us to the top of the hill in Bodø to look out at the Lofoten Islands before it got dark at 3 p.m. The fog wisped back and forth on the turbulent North Sea, obscuring the western view out to sea. "Well, the Lofoten Islands are out there somewhere," Magne told us as he pointed west. "They really are beautiful."

The fog turned into snowflakes that found their way to the ground. Magne smiled broadly and announced, "Now we have the snow, and that is good." As he drove us back to our hotel in downtown Bodø, the flurries became a blizzard. The sides of the road were indecipherable, but Magne was unfazed by the whiteout. The wipers of his Volvo violently brushed away the ice from his windshield. Magne grinned and told us that he was happy that he could show us a true northern Norwegian snowstorm.

Once we made it to the hotel, there was little to do except watch the swirling snow blow sideways down the deserted streets as we sipped cup after cup of complimentary hot chocolate. The sun had already set, but the town was bright white.

My parents risked the storm to walk through Bodø and do some sightseeing in a whiteout. Within minutes, they came back into the hotel covered in snow and afraid they'd blow away into the fjord.

Katy, Eilif, and I bundled up in our hotel room and watched Norwegian TV for the first time, since we didn't have a television in our apartment. We discovered why everyone spoke English so well: American television shows aren't dubbed as in most European countries. We wanted an escape from the blizzard outside but ended up watching *Seven Years in Tibet* in the snow-covered Himalayas.

Just when we were all ready to sleep, Katy discovered that we were out of diapers. She pointed out that I was the one who had pushed for a trip to northern Norway, so here was my chance to prove what a tough Scandinavian I was. I had little choice but to venture into the blizzard.

At 10 p.m., I pushed open the hotel door and walked into whiteness. The icy snow stung my face, so I involuntarily shut my eyes. Holding my hands over my face to keep out the wind, I squinted to see the slight shadows that were the buildings on both sides of the road. Stores were closed, and I was the only person on the streets of Bodø.

Visions of Jack London stories plagued my thoughts. Didn't that guy try to cut his dog open to warm his hands in "To Build a Fire"? How did he survive seventy below temperatures? Oh wait, he didn't. Good thing I don't have a dog, I thought. Even though I was in the middle of town, I knew we'd have a disaster on our hands if I didn't find diapers.

I saw a warm glow emanating from behind frosted windows. In spite of the blizzard, or perhaps because of it, pubs were packed with people. I spied a Turkish diner that was getting ready for the revelers after the bars closed. Smoke from fried onions and kabobs billowed out the exhaust pipe, mingled with the snow, and was blown through the streets of town to lure in customers. Using English and broken Norwegian, I asked the cook if he knew where I could buy diapers. He didn't understand, so I resorted to mime. I saw a look of pity in his eyes as he watched me: a grown man who just walked in from a snowstorm, pulling up imaginary pants and pretending to cry. He called to his coworker in the back room to come watch me. Before I further humiliated myself, I remembered my Norwegian dictionary in my pocket. I showed him the word for diaper. Ahh! He laughed and pointed down the street into the oblivion of the night.

I stepped out the door into the wall of white and saw the hazy light of a late-night Norwegian convenience store. The wind pushed me violently to the left toward the tumultuous North Sea, so I had to lean hard to the right to go straight toward my goal of diapers. I trudged up the icy steps and through a three-foot snowdrift to the glass doors of the store. I saw my reflection in the window: a snow blob with legs. When I pushed the door open and felt the blast of dry heat, it was almost as shocking as the cold.

The clerk, chatting away on his cell phone, barely acknowledged the snowdrift that had just entered. I was just another routine Arctic customer: a man with frozen eyelashes, possibly frostbitten, entering a store in a dangerous blizzard. The Bodø convenience store was loaded with firewood, potatoes, heavy bread, *lompe* (lefse), chocolate, and marzipan. Five flavors of cod liver oil filled the shelves: plain, lemon, orange, cherry, and fresh unflavored Lofoten oil. The metal "beer curtain" was closed to keep any intoxicating beverages out of the hands of revelers after dark.

I found the diapers right below the reindeer meat baby food with a drawing of a happy reindeer on the jar. I grabbed a bag of Pampers and paid my Norwegian kroner. The teenaged clerk didn't even stop his conversation on his cell phone as he rang me up. As I pushed open the door, I thought that he could be the last person I ever saw. He wouldn't even say good-bye.

A large group of revelers were singing heartily outside as they paraded through the snowstorm to get some late-night snacks. Since it was dark most of the time in the winter anyway, I supposed this was the equivalent of staying up all night in the summer, when the sun never sets.

As I passed this merry group, they waved happily and encouraged me to come along on their movable feast. I held up the bag of diapers, and they understood that I was on a mission.

The next morning, the blizzard had stopped, and quiet reigned. Eilif woke up at his usual 5:30, so we bundled up to go on an early morning walk through town. Last night's cold and wind were gone, replaced by silence. The snow absorbed all sound and froze time and space. As we laid down the first tracks through the street, we spoke softly as though our voices would crack this crystallized town.

When we returned to the hotel, my parents were already down at the breakfast buffet, enjoying three kinds of herring, mackerel in tomato sauce, shrimp spread, mayonnaise, sliced tomatoes and cucumbers, Jarlsberg cheese, fresh bread, waffles with whipped cream and strawberries, and lots of butter. Apart from coffee, tea, and juice to drink, several kinds of milk were offered along with two flavors of drinkable yogurt and buttermilk. My dad was in heaven as he discovered that his infamous "Norwegian dinners" back home were standard breakfast fare in Norway. Magne and Rigmor joined us for the meal; apparently the unplowed streets were just another fun challenge for Magne's Volvo.

Katy had lost the key to our hotel room. She searched all her pockets but had to go to the receptionist for another one. Rigmor told us that her forgetfulness was caused by *ammetåke*, the breast-feeding fog that affects all new mothers. It can last for months, she warned, and some mothers never quite get their memory back. Katy came back downstairs minutes later and told us that she had left the key in the door with a ten kroner coin in the key ring. Nobody had touched it.

Just then, I realized I didn't have my wedding ring on my finger. I ran up to our room to see if I had taken it off when I shaved that morning. I scoured the room but couldn't find it. Back at the breakfast table, I broke the news of the missing ring. No one was alarmed except for me. I looked nervously at Katy, who I thought might take it as an ominous sign, but she calmly said, "Well, we must find it."

Rigmor comforted me that I had probably just misplaced it. "Men can get the *ammetåke* too," she assured me. I wasn't quite sure how I could be in a breast-feeding fog, but lack of sleep surely made me forgetful. We left the herring breakfast behind and began to search.

For the next hour, we retraced our steps through the hotel and then our foot tracks through Bodø. Could my gloves have pulled the ring off when we were on the walk? Maybe it fell off last night when I went out in the blizzard. If the ring had fallen off in the snow, I knew the search was pointless, but we had to try.

The sun rose at 10:30 and sparkled off the millions of snowflakes. I wanted no part of this winter wonderland and just wanted to find the ring. As we searched, I thought about gloomy warnings relatives had given us: "You know many people get divorced when they have a child with colic." And "I never knew that Eric wanted to have children." As we searched in vain, Katy tried to reassure me—and herself—that we could get another ring like it when we got back to Minnesota. We looked at each other, wondering what this all meant.

Empty-handed, we went back to the hotel for some hot cocoa. Magne met us at the door. Somewhat stoically, he told me that the hotel staff had found my ring under our breakfast table when they were cleaning up the herring. I gave Katy a big hug and told her that I'd known we would find it. Besides, it's just a ring and not our marriage, right? For the first time in my life, my dad gave me stern advice that I should never ever take off my wedding ring. Katy feigned anger and warned, "Yeah, don't you ever take off that ring again."

The Knitting Hall of Fame

When Eilif was born, distant Norwegian relatives gathered together to knit elaborate sweaters for the new little Viking. Just a month after hearing of the birth, a seventy-five-year-old woman named Ingeborg from the town of Bjørk sent us a thick sweater of the local Lusterfjord pattern with deep blues, ruddy reds, and some mustard yellows. Again we heard the saying "In Norway, babies are born with skis, the parents provide the poles." The rest of the relatives knit the sweaters.

Each region of Norway has a different style of sweater—similar to the different tartan patterns in Scotland. Bergen has the Fana pattern with stripes, Selbu invented the star and animal motif, and Voss has the classic yoked design. Besides *bunads* (the hand-embroidered folk costumes worn for formal occasions and country dances), the typical Norwegian outfit is a hand-knit sweater with matching hat, gloves, and knee-high socks that go up to where the wool knickers begin. Nowadays, this getup is mostly seen on cross-country skiers.

Some Norwegians cringe at this quaint stereotype that they all run around in handmade sweaters and pass their time knitting. When my friend Astrid found out I was writing about Norway, she said, "That's great! Then you can dispel all the myths that Americans have of us that we go around in Norwegian sweaters and *bunads*." She confessed, however, to owning a *bunad* and a closet full of hand-knit sweaters. When winter came and almost all cross-country skiers wore this outfit, Astrid couldn't deny that it was the best outfit for skiing.

Other Norwegians want to preserve and honor this traditional craft of knitting intricate sweaters. A town named Selbu—outside of Trondheim—had a knitting circle of women famous throughout Norway because they developed their own patterns and were able to support themselves on knitting. In honor of these knitting revolutionaries, Selbu now boasts the Knitting Museum and Knitting Hall of Fame.

In the center of Trondheim, a military museum features mannequins of famous Norwegian resistance fighters during World War II, all wearing heavy Norwegian sweaters. The bright colors and patterns of these sweaters didn't offer much camouflage and probably made them easy targets for ruthless Nazis. Nevertheless, the Norwegian fighters certainly looked festive and cozy in their beautiful sweaters, especially next to the drab storm troopers from Düsseldorf.

In elementary school, Norwegian children have knitting class to help with coordination, mathematics, and relaxation. The knitting propaganda even extended to jaded college students, whom I saw riding the bus to class, clicking their knitting needles as their iPod headphones blared Metallica into their eardrums.

Entrepreneurial Norwegians translated this skill into a career. One woman set up a stand in the center of Trondheim to sell her homemade socks, gloves, and hats. This was a common sight especially around Christmas, when the women vied for position on the busiest street corners. One woman sold me the most expensive pair of wool socks I'd ever bought, but they were also the warmest.

Since Eilif had colic the first five months of life, we desperately needed a way to calm our nerves after all the fussing. Katy took up knitting as a way to relax. In the center of Trondheim, she stopped at one of the many knitting stores where women gathered to knit complicated sweaters while they chatted and drank strong coffee. I had high hopes that Katy's persistence would someday land her a coveted position in the Knitting Hall of Fame in Selbu. I envisioned the noble knitting council bestowing upon her the shining gilded knitting needles, and then her handprint being cemented into the future knitting walk of fame. My son and I would brag that we were there that fateful day she took up the needles and yarn to work her woolen magic.

To achieve this glory, Katy had to begin somewhere. The women at the knitting store showed her some basic Norwegian sweater designs. "It's really very easy," they insisted. Katy, who had never knit a stitch in her life, wisely chose to begin with a simple one-color red scarf. Back home in our apartment, she set the Norwegian instruction book on her lap, cast on, and began knitting and purling while the baby cooed jealously. I kept Eilif distracted, fed, and clothed with clean diapers, while Katy tried desperately to relax with her new hobby.

Full-color photos of luscious sweaters from her knitting book spurred her on, while black-and-white line drawings attempted to explain each step of the way. Armed with her Norwegian-English dictionary, she deciphered the text but had to set down her needles each time a new word stumped her. The loops slipped off the needles, and some stitches were snug while others loose. To even it out, she stretched what little she had done. Just then the baby grabbed the ball of yarn with his vicelike grip and pulled with all his might. The little scarf tightened up in a ball.

So much for relaxation. In a rage, Katy threw the yarn and needles across the room. The baby rolled over to them for a taste. Since the plastic needles were dull, we let him play with them to keep him quiet. When we noticed his whole mouth and chin covered in red, we ran to the rescue. Snatching away the knitting needles, we realized Eilif was fine. He was chewing on her red yarn and cried when we wouldn't let him keep eating it.

Katy occasionally picked up the needles again, but the relaxation promised by her guidebook never washed over her. After numerous false starts, broken yarn, and unwound knitting (thanks to the baby's powerful grip), Katy hung up her knitting needles — at least until the baby was in college. With only two inches finished of her scarf, Katy's knitting career had come to an abrupt end. Perhaps as part of her master plan, however, she somehow convinced her friend Margaret, who had come for a visit, to knit the entire red scarf for the baby.

Døping the Baby

We wanted to baptize Eilif in Nidaros, Trondheim's cathedral, which dates back to 1070. The entrance features a lineup of famous bloody martyrs — some holding the beheaded skulls of monks in a basket. The massive stone church is the dominant building in town and has survived fires, a conversion from Catholicism, and the Danes' looting of St. Olaf's remains. Gargoyles menace pilgrims from the eaves, and the dark interior of the church is dimly lit through gigantic stained-glass windows. While not exactly a baby-friendly environment, Nidaros seemed appropriate for two parents with a colicky baby.

We weren't worried that our unbaptized baby would end up in Limbo (even the Pope had recently questioned its existence) or whether he would be Catholic, Lutheran, or Presbyterian. Both Katy and I were raised going to church, but our skeptical nature didn't convince us that baptizing our baby would save him from damnation. However, if we didn't baptize Eilif in Norway, our relatives at home would insist on doing it in their churches (where priests would warn of fire and brimstone lest we change our ways).

At the rectory of Nidaros, the church secretary told us that our baby would have to be put on a waiting list — on standby in case another baby couldn't show up. The rector recommended that we speak with the Anglican priest who gave an English service twice a month in Nidaros.

An English woman, who was a sort of priest-in-training and assistant to the Anglican preacher, called us up the next day and insisted on paying us a visit to discuss the baptism. Because of our new baby, our house was in no shape for a visit by a priest. Besides, what exactly did we have to discuss about pouring a bit of water over the baby's head?

Katy and I traded off rocking the baby as we struggled to clean our disaster of an apartment. The diapers were cleaned, the toys put away, and the spit-up mopped off the floor.

Florence showed up fifteen minutes early, wearing a practical tweed skirt and buttoned-up blouse with a pink ribbon tied as a sort of cravat. Even though the sky was clear, she carried an umbrella looped over her right arm, along with a black mackintosh. "You never know," she explained.

I took her raincoat and umbrella, and she waited patiently in the cramped entranceway. "Come on in," I said and gestured to the living room (which is the only room besides the bedroom, kitchen, or bathroom).

"Where shall I sit?" she asked politely.

"Anywhere you want," Katy replied.

"I shall sit here then." Florence chose her seat, whisked her arm under her skirt to avoid creasing the fabric, and sat with perfect posture. I offered her something to drink: coffee, *ingefærøl* (good strong Norwegian ginger ale), Solo (orange juice soda)...

"Do you have any tea?" she asked hopefully.

I was worried she'd ask for tea because she probably knew full well Americans can't make it properly. (Was this retaliation for the Boston Tea Party?) I had no hot-water kettle, tea cozy, loose Ceylon tea, or even a teapot. Instead, I heated water in a pan and plopped a teabag of Earl Grey in a coffee-stained cup. "I hope this is OK," I said half-heartedly.

"I'm sure it's divine," she replied.

"What is your religion?" Florence asked. Katy explained that each one of our parents came from different denominations, but we were married at a Lutheran church by a Presbyterian minister.

"Isn't that different?" she replied. I knew to keep my mouth shut since I almost derailed our marriage when I got into an existential conversation with the minister two weeks before the ceremony.

When Florence found out we didn't make it to church

much, she stated that it was important to reaffirm our faith. She could help us.

Eilif began fussing, so Katy and I traded off standing up to rock the baby energetically in our arms to calm him down. Florence didn't seem to notice Eilif's loud crying, and asked us the religion of the godparents. We'd asked our Norwegian friends Knut and Inger to be godparents, but we never thought to ask them their religion. Florence wanted to be certain that they would raise our baby in a strict Christian way.

After an hour and a half of questions about our beliefs and the religion of our friends and family, Florence decided it was time to go home and make supper. I noticed that she had only taken a sip of her tea and hadn't touched any cookies. "I'd like to come back soon so we can chat again. We have prayer groups that gather once a week, and you can meet many other English-speakers. They're really quite fun."

"Before I go," Florence continued, "I'd like to say a prayer for the baby." Katy looked at me nervously. Florence bowed her head solemnly, put her hands together, and called on the Lord to bless this new family. For the first time, she paid attention to the baby and reached her hand toward him. "And please help Eilif recover from his colic." After an uncomfortable silence, she lifted her head, opened her eyes, and said, "That was nice. I can't wait to come back for another visit."

Katy quickly fetched her raincoat and umbrella. Florence seemed uncomfortable when I offered to shake her hand but said happily, "Good-bye now! Farewell! Toodle-oo!" I opened the door for her, and a cloudburst had just started to soak the dirt streets. "See, I knew it was going to rain," she said and marched out, avoiding the puddles.

"Well, that was a disaster," Katy said, and I breathed a sigh of relief that she agreed that we didn't have to see Florence again. The baptism was delayed indefinitely, and we considered telling all the relatives that Eilif was already baptized so we didn't have to deal with another Florence.

A couple of weeks later on our daily walk downtown to the fish market, we passed by the Lademoen church with its stone spires overlooking a little neighborhood park. It was March, and the snow melted one day only to be replaced by ice the next. As we circled around the massive stone building, Katy asked me if we should check into this church for the possibility of a baptism. If we ran into Florence again, we could tell her that we wanted to use our neighborhood church.

We carried Eilif in his stroller up the steps and pulled the massive iron handle. The door was open. Inside the chapel, Eilif gazed up at the gold stars painted on the vaulted sky-blue ceiling.

Hilde, the minister, was in her office and welcomed us to sit down. She giggled and apologized for the mess of papers covering her desk and her "inadequate English" (which was perfect). She felt around for her glasses so she could take a good look at the baby. Eilif had dozed off, so for once we could sit and relax. In fact, we contemplated running home to take a nap while he slept. "He's so calm and peaceful like a little angel," she whispered, but I realized that she was speaking normally. I was wearing my industrial-strength earplugs to block Eilif's screams.

She offered us coffee and thin ginger snaps. The powerful and exciting Norwegian coffee seeped into our blood to snap us from our slumber. We explained that we wanted to have Eilif baptized in her church. Hilde wasn't concerned about our religious background or beliefs but was more interested in how we were getting along in Trondheim. Do you study at the university? Are you finding everything you need in town? Have you made some friends?

We chatted a bit but were nervous that Eilif was going to wake up and begin crying. Katy finally came out and asked if Hilde would be able to perform the baptism here in Lademoen. Katy cautioned her that Eilif could scare off all her congregation with his crying.

"It's OK if Eilif cries," she assured us, "that's just what babies do." She explained that in the baptism, right after she put water on the baby's head, she would hold him up above her to show him to the parishioners.

Katy gasped. "Oh no, that's not a good idea. See, he spits up a lot."

Hilde laughed. "Well, I have three children of my own, so it'll be OK. You do know that the whole service will be in Norwegian, of course."

Katy replied, "I don't really want to understand what they're saying because then I probably wouldn't go through with it." We both remembered other baptisms in which the minister proclaimed that the holy water was a blow against Satan and now the Devil could not lay his hands on this baby.

"Do we have to say anything?" I asked.

"I will just ask you his name, and I'll make a gesture to you about that, and then you say, 'Eilif.' Then I'll ask you if you'd like him to be baptized, and you say . . . at least I hope you'll say 'yes.'" Hilde hesitated. "But that's up to you since you can always change your mind."

"By the way, the day of the baptism will also be a children's service." Hilde laughed. "It can be a bit crazy because the youth group will perform much of the ceremony, apart from the baptism."

Later that day we told Eilif's future Norwegian godparents, Knut and Inger, about the date. Inger couldn't come to the baptism because her nephew was being baptized the same day out of town. Knut would attend alone, and I could tell he wasn't crazy about the idea of going to church. When I told him that it would be a children's mass too, all he said was, "Oh no, it will be utter chaos."

In spite of being up half the night with the baby, we managed to iron our clothes to look presentable. We didn't dare press the fragile one-hundred-year-old christening gown that had been sent to Norway and had been worn by Katy and everyone else in her family for generations.

With foam plugs fit snugly into our ears, Katy and I pushed the baby in his buggy to the church. The sun had made it over the hills, and Eilif calmed down when he got some fresh air. It was late April, and the days were already long with lazy sunrises and sunsets that treated us with hours of pink skies.

Knut met us outside the church and laughed when he saw Eilif wrapped in a huge blue-and-white checkered bib (actually our little tablecloth from our picnic basket) so he couldn't spit up on the precious christening gown. "He looks more like he's going to eat spaghetti in an Italian restaurant than be baptized," Katy admitted.

The ceremony began with a procession of children, nervous youngsters in front of the feisty teenagers. Two kids with low-rider pants, ripped band T-shirts, and chains clanging at their side caused a gaggle of older women to murmur excitedly to each other through cupped hands. One of them shrugged as if to say it was better the kids were in church after all. A few elementary schoolkids managed to lose their way down the aisle, resulting in others unsuccessfully stifling their giggles. Hilde helped them find their way to the altar and averted the predicted chaos.

A priest from Sierra Leone took the podium as the guest preacher to this all-white Lutheran congregation. In perfect Norwegian, he belted out his sermon with a thunderous baritone. Slowly, his voice rose, and his arms pumped in rhythm with his words. I understood a few words: salvation, God, and brotherly love. He pulled the microphone from the stand, strutted across the altar preaching the word, and pointed to the congregation to join him in his faith. The elderly women near the front fidgeted in their seats and put their heads back as though to distance themselves. One of them slumped down behind her pew for protection. His sermon ended with his arms in the air and a sung "Hallelujah!"

Knut whispered to me, "Obviously, he was trying to get some enthusiasm, but that's nearly impossible from a Norwegian congregation."

Hilde took the podium, and the old women breathed easily and sat up straight again. As she announced that we were going to have a special baptism today, Eilif spat up down my sleeve all the way to my elbow. My white shirt hid the mess, but a puddle formed in the elbow and slowly dripped spit-up underneath me. I smelled the cod liver oil, but Eilif was happy now that his stomach felt better.

Hilde didn't notice and just saw a smiling baby. She gently talked to the congregation in Norwegian and then turned to us. Katy and I smiled back at her, but she just kept looking at us expectantly. We relished the event in this airy church under a ceiling of gold stars. I wanted to remember this moment when our son was being baptized in this beautiful church. Hilde gestured to me in anticipation. Knut then elbowed me, "You're supposed to say, '*Ja!*'"

"Oh, *ja, ja*, yes, yes, we do!" I said hurriedly.

Hilde breathed now and poured water over Eilif's head as I continued to hold him. The cool water ran over his head, down my arm, and washed out my sleeve. She read a passage from her Bible, and Eilif quickly reached out and grabbed the book. She had a good grip on it, however, and easily won the tug-of-war.

Hilde then took Eilif into her hands to hold him up above her head to get a good look at him. This was the moment I'd been dreading for weeks, the scene playing in slow motion in my head. I imagined he'd spit up what was left in his stomach, and we'd have to leave the country the next day or have him go through an exorcism.

Hilde carefully held up Eilif to face her but not directly above her head — she'd obviously done this before. They looked at each other for a moment, and Eilif reached out to grab her glasses. She was quick enough to avoid his hands. Instead he got a good tuft of her graying hair and gave it a yank. She was a pro and pretended not to notice. Eilif hung on to the clump of hair and stared attentively at Hilde while she talked to him and the congregation. When she took a breath, Eilif decided to give his own sermon. He mimicked her by preaching to the crowd, "Blah, blah, blah, blah." The little old ladies in front chuckled.

She presented Eilif to the congregation, and he giggled. Afterwards, a couple of elderly women crowded around to pinch his cheeks. They told everyone to come to the back of the airy sanctuary for coffee and marzipan cake that had been laid out on card tables.

A few of the little old ladies came up to wish us all the best; at least I think that was what they said. I could understand some basic Norwegian, but when I heard the local dialect, *Trøndersk,* I was lost. I thanked them gratefully, "*Takk skal du ha.*" One of them just shook her head and pointed to the spit-up on my sleeve that was dripping on to the floor.

In Cod We Trust

"My relatives assure me that it is indeed the most beautiful place on earth," Margaret told us. Rather than being blocked off from the sun and sky by fjords, the Lofoten Islands boast the opposite landscape. Sharp snow-covered rugged mountains pierce the low-flying clouds, and the wide-open North Sea, or the blue meadow, as Norwegians sometimes call it, gives breathing space for claustrophobics tired of the stifling deep valleys of the fjords. Painters travel to these islands for the expansive sunsets that stretch for hours in every shade of blue, yellow, and pink. Copying the colorful sky and the light bouncing off the snow and water would look garish and unbelievable, so I imagined the frustrated artists laid down their brushes just to watch.

Fog from the North Sea had shrouded the Lofoten Islands the last time we had tried to see them from across the channel in Bodø. Now, we spent an entire day traveling by turbulent plane and sickening boat to the islands made famous by the giant schools of cod that encircled them. At last Katy, Margaret, baby Eilif, and I had an excuse to go: to visit Margaret's relatives.

Margaret is Katy's best friend from Minnesota and fits a Norwegian stereotype: tall, thin, with very fair skin and long blonde hair. Randi-Kristine, Margaret's cousin in the Lofoten Islands, on the other hand, is shorter, stout, with dark hair and has an almost gothic look, which fits her occupation of writing period romances.

At first I thought Randi-Kristine's claim that the Lofoten Islands are "the world's most beautiful place" was her literary exaggeration, but Norway is full of hyperbole: the city of Tromsø calls itself "the Paris of the North," the town of Henningsvær claims it's "the Venice of the Lofoten," and the Hurtigruten ferry trip up the coast of Norway is "the world's most beautiful voyage." In a country where the people seem low key, reserved, and loathe to exaggerate, they overstate with a straight face. When I questioned these claims, the response was, "Well, where is the 'Paris of the North' if it isn't Tromsø?" or "Can you find me a more beautiful trip than up the Norwegian coastline?"

Mostly, I had been excited to feast on the famous cod from the sea around the islands. Cod is called the "beefsteak of the sea" and was one of the pillars of the Norwegian economy before the discovery of oil and natural gas. A century ago when my great-grandfather Ellef was still in the Sognefjord, more than half of the fish consumed in Europe was cod, most of it from Norway. Today, the giant cod, which can be four feet long, are fewer from overfishing. I'd read about the giant schools of spawning cod that the fishermen would net; the added weight of the fish sometimes capsized their boats. The women waited on shore, hoping that the men would return from the dangerous fishing trips. If and when the boats returned, the fishwives would spend an entire week cutting up the bounty of cod.

When we arrived, Randi-Kristine was preparing a special dinner for us, but she wasn't quite ready to serve up the special Lofoten feast. Margaret had met Randi-Kristine a few years before during a family reunion at the Holiday Inn in Fargo, North Dakota. Now Randi-Kristine was showing us true Norwegian hospitality as she diligently prepared the table and put the finishing touches on her Norwegian spread. Meanwhile, her thirteen-year-old son Jarl-Andre showed us around the tiny coastal town with deserted streets. Jarl-Andre pointed out the sites: a small store, a little newspaper kiosk in an old wooden house, and a little *kro* restaurant that is open only on special occasions. "We even have a taxi! Just like New York," he bragged as he pointed to a parked car.

"A taxi?" Margaret asked. "Why do you need a taxi when you can walk everywhere in town?"

"It's mostly to drive the old women into the big town of Svolvær to go shopping," he replied and described how the taxi would wait outside the stores as the women would linger over tea with friends and then stuff the cab full of food for the month.

Maybe twenty houses were perched along the coast of Randi-Kristine's town, and all seemed to be gathered together for one reason: the fish processing plant. "You might want to hold your nose now because we will be passing the drying fish," Jarl-Andre warned us. On top of hills and out on windy jetties, large wooden A-framed racks that reached thirty feet into the air were hung with drying cod carcasses. Fishing boats pulled up to the large cement building where crates of fresh fish were unloaded. The doors swung freely to bring in the breeze from the sea as the fish were systematically beheaded and their entrails ripped out. The meat of the cod was hung out to make *tørfisk*, dried fish, which would easily keep for twenty years. The drying fish dangled from clotheslines, sign-posts, and even mailboxes in town. Sometimes the fish was salted at the same time and then dried out on the rocks to make jerkylike snacks called *klippefisk*. Within six to twelve weeks, 85 percent of the water would evaporate, making a piece of fish cardboard that could be soaked in water for supper just like the Vikings did centuries before.

I asked Jarl-Andre if the seagulls circling overhead peck at the fish.

"Oh, they do; that's why some fishermen put nets over the fish to stop them," he explained. "People even steal the fish too."

The tastiest meat of cod is supposedly around the fish's jaw, the back of the neck, and the tongue. Children in Norwegian fishing villages could make extra money cutting out cod tongues for Christmas dinners. "Yuck. Why would I want to do that?" Jarl-Andre said and pointed to thousands of fish heads strung together and swinging in the wind from a drying rack. He explained that these heads are ground up and sold to markets in China for soup stock. Jarl-Andre was happy riding his BMX bike and wanted nothing to do with fish.

Katy and Margaret had lost their appetites, but I was starving for some fresh fish for dinner. We arrived back at the house just as Randi-Kristine was putting supper on the table. Rather than a giant fish fillet, however, she had roasted a turkey for the American guests. She described how it was difficult to find a turkey on the Lofoten Islands; she had to special order it weeks before.

"We don't eat much fish," she said, "and I'd never serve it to guests."

I tried not to show my disappointment, but I asked if it was true that most Norwegian households eat fish five to six times a week. She couldn't believe that and said their family didn't like fish. She told us maybe she wasn't typically Norwegian since "I don't very much like winter," which seemed unfortunate considering she was living in the Arctic.

Randi-Kristine told how she'd traveled to the Midwest of the United States to visit Margaret and other relatives, but one of the most memorable trips was visiting friends in a small town in Iowa for an annual Norwegian American festival. With her writerly flair, she described the parade down main street of all the people in old Norwegian *bunader* and folk costumes. She and her family laughed when they heard the nationalistic anthems that the marching chorus was belting out proudly. "They were singing songs in Swedish!" she said. When she informed them, they insisted, "No, they're in Norwegian!" Otherwise the proud Norwegian Americans would have had to admit that all these years they'd been singing in the language of their questionable neighbors.

In spite of her dislike of the cold and cod of northern Norway, Randi-Kristine and her family were hesitant to ever leave their beloved Lofoten Islands. (They pronounced it LOO-fow-ten with a dramatic bob of the head emphasizing each syllable.)

But even the warm endless days of summer present adverse conditions. Tourists arrive on the islands for the summer solstice to see the *midnattsol*. Randi-Kristine warned that when they see the midnight sun, there are very few clouds overhead, and the sea is calm. Although everyone believes this is good luck, the next day the sea rebels, a storm blows in, and the horrible *midnattsolvind* (midnight sun wind) sweeps over the islands. Even in the face of good omens, islanders are wary of the sea.

After our Norwegian thanksgiving feast, Randi-Kristine dropped us off at our rented fisherman's cabin, a *rorbu*, that was propped up on stilts above the waterline in the town of Svolvær. "Imagine how it used to smell in there!" Randi-Kristine said. "There used to be about twenty sailors who would sleep in a *rorbu*. Now the fishermen don't actually live in *rorbuer;* they live in their boats, which are totally modern with stoves, television, and other things." I couldn't understand how much more modern our *rorbu* could be since it had been renovated with electricity, plumbing, and a little kitchenette.

I'd heard how the brave Lofoten fishermen would sleep in their work clothes, which constantly smelled like fish, and often wouldn't change their clothes all winter. (Legend is fishermen kept these habits when they left for the lumber camps in northern Minnesota. In the spring, they'd probably just peel off the long underwear—or shave it off—and toss it in the fire.) At this point, I was used to the fishy smell of the sea.

Our shaky wooden *rorbu* was immaculate and cozy with a view of Svolvær's center across the small bay and a mountain with the "Goat's Horn," two precarious crags a yard and a half apart that brave climbers jump across. I had been hoping that our little red cabin would have a fishing hole in the floor like some of them do, so we could catch dinner when the tide rose under the floor. Katy didn't even like the idea of fishing from our balcony into the shallow water that washes in all sorts of debris after the ebb tide. To add to her skepticism about fishing from home, Margaret pointed out that the sewage pipes from our toilet went under the cabin and out about forty feet into the water, where a patch of seaweed flourished.

The fresh salty smell of the sea permeated the cabin, and occasionally a whiff of fish passed through the cabin. Katy gave me a suspicious look as if to question if I'd been fishing or sneaked some old cod into our tiny cabin. We realized where the smell originated during a walk farther out on the rocky point of Svinøya. Giant racks of drying cod were set up around a small fish processing plant. Purring cats full of tidbits lay on the sunny rocks as seagulls dive-bombed disposed fish entrails. Baby Eilif mimicked the cawing of the gulls, and I pointed out that he was hungry for fish, too.

Next to the A-frame racks of drying fish, destroyed Nazi bunkers were wedged between the rocks, built when the Germans had tried to hold on to this strategic port in the North Atlantic. These lonesome islands were a combat zone during World War II, and earlier when foreign ships fought over the abundant fish. Even today, one of the reasons Norway doesn't want to enter the European Union is because it doesn't want to open up its famed fishing waters.

Thirty thousand men once worked as fishermen off the Lofoten Islands and tried to sail home to these little *rorbuer.* The owners of the huts often treated them like indentured servants. When given the chance, they hopped ship and immigrated to America like my great-grandfather did.

Margaret told me about her great-great-grandmother who left the Lofoten Islands supposedly because the fishing boat of her betrothed was swallowed by the furious waves of the sea. She was not alone. Today, a lone fish widow statue at the end of the point looks sadly out to the sea that killed her husband.

The next morning, I resolved to eat a fantastic fish dinner. We walked into Svolvær and scouted the restaurants. Pizzerias, bakeries, and stands selling *pølser,* hot dogs, were easy to find, but fish restaurants were curiously absent. A restaurant named "Bacalao" after the famous Mediterranean cod dish in tomato sauce was serving liquor but no fish today. Finally on the harbor, we found a fancy restaurant that served fresh fish—but no cod—and "whale tartar," which was yet another reason that Norway didn't want to join the E.U.: whaling would be banned. A meal at this restaurant would cost nearly as much as our travel from Trondheim to the island, so I told Katy and Margaret that we could find a fish shop and cook the best fish dinner in town in the kitchenette of our *rorbu*.

Two older men who looked like ex-fishermen with blue caps and thick wool shirts strolled along the waterfront. One of them squeaked with each step in his rubber Wellington boots. The other man puffed a pipe leisurely and blew the smoke upwards to create a cloud overhead.

I asked them if there was a good place to buy fish in Svolvær.

"You mean to eat?" the man with a pipe asked.

"Well, yes . . ." I replied, unsure of what else I would do with a fish.

"Hmmm. You can go to the little Rimi store two blocks away," the man in galoshes said, referring to a large grocery chain.

The smoking man interrupted, "But it's not so fresh. Don't go there."

The man with the pipe said, "We don't have a proper fish shop here. It's very difficult to buy good fish here."

"You don't have a fish shop?" I asked. "I thought that we could find the freshest fish in the world in Lofoten." I was being far too confrontational, as the men were a bit taken aback by my insistence. They seemed disturbed that I was pressing them, so they changed topic and asked what kind of fish I wanted. "Cod," I replied simply.

"There are many different kinds of cod," the man in boots pointed out. He counted on his fingers as he listed them, "You have *torsk, kolmule, sei, brosme, kolje, lysing, lange, lyr, hvitting,* and *skrei* is winter cod, and *kysttorsk* is coastal cod. Which do you want?"

The other man added, "And do you want smoked *torsk*, salt *torsk*, dried *torsk*, fish balls, or fresh *torsk*?"

I could see they were trying to distract me from my objective, but I pressed on. "It doesn't really matter what kind of fish, as long as it's fresh."

As though to get me off their backs, the man in galoshes said, "You can go to see some of the boats coming in and ask them." He pointed down the pier to a cement building along the water.

We walked down there to find a boat unloading, but the fish were all at least three feet long. I asked the fisherman in my broken Norwegian if we could buy some fish for dinner. My Norwegian seemed to confuse him as he shook his head. All his fish were already sold. Besides, what would we do with a ten-pound cod? I couldn't clean this giant fish in our hotel room without causing an international incident.

In the end, we ended up at the fish counter of the little Rimi grocery store. She had perfectly fresh cod but told me that we would be much more pleased with the fish balls or fish pudding.

"Fish pudding?" I asked, a bit disgusted.

"It's very tasty," she replied, pointing to a small white loaf next to the cod fillets. "We use ground haddock with cornstarch and heavy cream. It's delicious!"

I said that we could try it another time, but we'd like the cod fillets. She grudgingly packaged up the fish for us. I didn't know whether she wanted it for herself, or if she was truly concerned about what we would like best.

Victorious, we brought our booty back to the *rorbu* and made a fantastic fish lunch with new potatoes on the side. I relished each bite of the delicate white meat with a sprinkle of lemon and parsley on top. Katy picked at her plate but ate it slowly. She then gave her judgment, "You know that I don't really like cod, don't you? It's just sort of bland. I much prefer salmon." I wasn't going to be bothered. I had found cod and understood why boats risked the dangerous waves to scoop up the fish that spawned here from the Barents Sea farther north. We ate our prized fish on the sunny balcony over the bay that looked out over the North Sea, which was calm for once.

Syttende Mai: Constitution Day

"Playing my baritone at 6 a.m. to wake people up on this happy day is what *syttende mai* is all about for me," said Sissel, my Norwegian teacher. "People don't mind because they want to get the most out of the day as possible."

Every day from December 21 to June 21 adds about six more minutes of daylight. Spring is in full swing by May Day, but the biggest celebration is Constitution Day on the seventeenth of May, or *syttende mai*.

For this holiday, we traveled to southern Norway to stay with a Norwegian friend of my dad. Kari took seriously her responsibility to show us an authentic *syttende mai* in her town of Tønsberg. Now that we had survived the *mørketid*, it was once again time to bask in the sunlight.

Thankfully, the marching bands didn't wake me until 7:58 a.m., when the cannons went off.

At breakfast, Kari was already wearing her *bunad*, or "national costume," which she had ironed the previous week in anticipation of the big day. The colorful cross-stitching around the border of the dress was a floral bouquet that never wilted. Kari explained that each *bunad* came from a different region — Vestfold, Hardangerfjord, Sogn, Telemark, and so on — and joked that tight-fitting "*bunads* have special extensions because they shrink when you leave them in the closet all year."

For this important day, we would be typically underdressed in clothes wrinkled from being jammed in our suitcases. We had tried to wash our clothes the day before, but Kari warned us, "Don't hang your wash on a Sunday."

"What would happen?" I asked, confused.

"Well, I don't know," she replied. "I don't think anyone would say anything, but I'd rather not try it."

When I suggested we wash our clothes on the seventeenth of May, Kari shook her head. This is a holiday, after all.

By 9:30 a.m., Kari's usually quiet street was crowded with people walking downtown to see the *barnetoget,* or children's parade. During the union with Sweden, nationalistic Norwegian parades marking Constitution Day were banned until Norwegian poet Henrik Wergeland calculated that the Swedes couldn't stop children from marching and waving Norwegian flags. The children's parade came to symbolize not only Norwegian nonviolent protest of Swedish rule but Norway's dedication to peaceful solutions to world problems ever since the signing of the constitution in Eidsvoll, Norway, on the seventeenth of May 1814.

Back in Trondheim, some German classmates had been shocked by all the flags, which they considered dangerous nationalism. My Norwegian teacher, Sissel, defended that tradition: "I don't think of it as very nationalistic, but rather to be proud of my country for a day. It's not to exclude other people, like immigrants, because they take part in it too."

During this Constitution Day in Tønsberg, Norwegian flags dangled from every lamppost, and hundreds more were waved by everyone watching the children's parade. Eilif waved a little flag from his stroller at the kids passing. Patriotism was on display, and the lack of militarism plus pride in Norway made it a cause for celebration rather than exclusion. Even so, "there was much discussion whether people from other countries should be able to wave their country's flags," Kari said. "I don't think it's right. In Stavanger, they let people do it, but not in most places." She pointed out that sometimes you see the "herring salad" flag, so named because it's a mix of the Norwegian flag with the Swedish flag in the upper right-hand corner to represent the old occupation by Sweden.

The red-hatted Russ, the graduating high schoolers, kept the parade lighthearted as they infiltrated it with enormous neon squirt guns and mocking chants of "hip-hip-hip-hurrah!"

Some gave out Russ trading cards of themselves, which little kids gathered feverishly in admiration of these wild teenagers. Fueled with shopping carts full of Ringnes beer, the Russ gave fake bombastic speeches, sang off-color songs, and generally did whatever they wanted during this last celebration before adulthood.

Following the children's parade, the crowd headed for the stands selling *pølser* and formed a long line around the block. Norwegian even has a word for this phenomenon: *pølsekø*, or "queue for wieners." Kari assured me these sausages were specially prepared for the seventeenth of May and weren't the ordinary *pølser* found at convenience stores, known as *bensin-stasjonspølsene* (gas station wieners). The year before, Shell gas stations in Norway sold fifteen million wieners, and Total stations sold thirty-nine thousand tons of hot dogs. Today was the boom day for wieners, and most parents let kids eat as many as they wanted.

Apart from the hot dogs, I imagined this scene of adults chatting in their *bunader* had changed little from a hundred years ago. "*Syttende mai* has always been basically an excuse to talk with people in town," Kari said.

While everyone had a spring in their step on the way to the parade, the crowd slowed on the way home after spending the day in dress shoes. "I've brought some medication for blisters if you need it," Kari said. For once I was glad that I had underdressed for the occasion.

After meeting dozens of people whom I wouldn't recognize later without their *bunader,* we walked home to watch the *syttende mai* parade in Oslo on TV. Compared to the small-town parade in Tønsberg with gunnysack races and fishing for prizes at the local kindergarten, the formal hoopla in Oslo seemed stilted. Kari pointed to the television screen. "There's our king, the one with the sour face. I think we should do away with the royals! But then what would the tabloids have to write about?"

As we relaxed, neighbors popped by for a visit, and Kari apologized, "If I were to be proper, I should serve you whipped eggs with brandy. It's a *syttende mai* tradition, but I don't particularly like it." Instead we sat down for homemade *gravlaks* and were thankful that the long days of summer were here at last.

You Can't Eat Beauty

During the nineteenth century, most of Norway was cut off from the rest of Europe's industry and opulence; Norwegian villages struggled to keep the people fed on preserved fish and porridge. Ellef Drægni, my great-grandfather, came from the source of the Sognefjord, on one of the branches of the lengthy waterway called the Lusterfjord. His town was Fortun—ironically meaning "fortune" in English—on a freshwater lake past the end of the fjord.

To discover our long-lost ancestral home, Katy, baby Eilif, and I had to choose between taking the bus on the long twisty road that winds through the desolate highland over the highest mountain road in Norway or travel 127 miles up the Sognefjord on a leisurely boat and sleep at classic old hotels along the waterfront. I pushed for the treacherous Viking route above the tree line, which used to be marked only by rock cairns. These stacked stones were placed around the glaciers, frozen for centuries, leaking azure blue water. Katy looked at me blankly, and I knew we would travel by ferry up the fjord.

Ellef Drægni left Norway by this route for America. Giant snowdrifts falling from the glaciers in winter close the road over the mountains from October through April. The only way out of this rocky cage in the winter is via water—the narrow Lusterfjord to the Sognefjord to the North Sea and Bergen, Norway's largest Atlantic port. At eighteen, Ellef traveled alone to the rainy port city of Bergen and searched for a berth on a wooden ship. Ellef embarked on his voyage alone and would never see Norway or his parents again. I can imagine him on the creaky wooden sailboat eating hardtack and dried fish on the dangerous trip, sleeping in cramped quarters with Norwegian families, nervous about the life ahead of them.

Now we were retracing Ellef's path from Norway but in reverse. Traveling by train to Bergen, we descended into a cloud trapped by the mountains and covering the city. Our train had an entire car dedicated to children with a large jungle gym and kids' movies and storybooks to keep the youngsters happy.

We arrived during a downpour. Our backpacks, waterproof under normal conditions, were instantly soaked. As if they were ready for a fishing trip, schoolchildren walked happily past us wearing rubber Wellington boots, raincoats, and pants. Every puddle was an excuse to splash each other. We saw an umbrella vending machine, but we were already singing in the rain to entertain baby Eilif. We covered his stroller with a poncho and trudged through flooded cobblestone streets by the fish market to the pier and the boat that would take us up the fjord.

The captain of the boat, the *Fjord 1*, kept a steady monologue over the intercom of the boat as we floated along. "The Sognefjord is the longest and deepest fjord in the world, measuring three thousand feet deep. The water is as deep as the mountains are high . . ."

We wouldn't see houses along the fjord for an hour. The crystal water gave way to the dense green foliage on the banks, which rose nearly vertically to the rock cliffs topped with a whipping cream–like snowcap. As famous as the area is for its beauty, the population is very small and triples when the tourists arrive.

"On your right is the town of Vangsnes. You can see Fridtjof the Intrepid, the legendary Viking king of Sogn," read the captain from his speech. "It is the largest statue on the Sognefjord, standing twelve meters high, and was donated by Kaiser Wilhelm, who was a regular visitor to the area. The statue was built in Germany in fifteen pieces and weighs 14,000 kilograms." And here the captain deviated from the script: "So there's no way they can get rid of the monstrosity now!" The people on the boat laughed because they obviously shared his dislike of having an overbearing Viking statue, donated by the Germans, glorifying the Nordic past.

At the end of the Sognefjord, we entered the Lusterfjord to find my great-grandfather's birthplace, Fortun. Along the way, I recognized a modern mountain lodge, which I'd seen in an article, run by a Drægni. We stopped inside and asked the tall, forty-year-old blond guy at the reception if he knew the Drægni who owned the lodge. "That's me, I'm Ole Berger Drægni," he responded.

I had found a long-lost relative! I pulled him outside so we could get our photo taken together. Katy snapped photos as I commented how much we looked alike; we both had blond hair and blue eyes, but he stood a head taller than me.

Our great-grandfather Ellef was very dark, however, with piercing blue eyes. My dad told me about all the dark Norwegians with olive skin and black hair from the Luster and Sognefjord who met at the Minnesota State Fair. The myth in our family was that our great-great-etc.-grandmother came from Portugal, perhaps a damsel in distress captured on some Viking invasion of Lisbon.

"Didn't you know that the Spanish Armada was stranded off of Bergen?" Ole Berger asked. "They say it was either after a battle with the British and they came to hide in the Sognefjord, or that they just got lost. Many of the sailors liked Norway so much that they stayed."

I was pleased our long-lost relatives were not only Vikings but also conquistadors, who brought the much-talked-about "dark gene" to my family in Norway. These vicious knights in plate armor fell for stunning Norwegian lasses and laid down their warring ways to raise raspberries and eat lutefisk in the Sognefjord. Perhaps my great-great-great-grandmother was a Portuguese princess taken prisoner by the dastardly Spanish, then rescued and taken to Norway for safekeeping.

Ole Berger offered us jet-black Norwegian coffee and wild blueberry cake in his Turtagrø restaurant. His father — our distant uncle? — joined us, and it seemed as if he had just woken up after a rough night on a bar stool. They unrolled an old map of the Drægni farm in Fortun and showed us where everyone lived. I imagined some enormous old country estate with sweeping vistas of the fjords.

Pointing to the map, Ole Berger said, "This was the house of the people who went to America. There were many people living in this very small house along the river. It flooded and was ruined. Now it is gone, and they've put up a small garage instead." My dreams of reclaiming my mantle as the heir to the manor were fading.

"This was the main farmhouse where our relatives lived and still do," Ole Berger told us. "Then there were nine other houses, and your great-great-grandfather was a *husmann* (tenant farmer)." In other words, Ellef's family worked for his, and Ellef's father took the name of the farm: Drægni. Ole Berger looked me in the eye. "I definitely think we're not related."

He told us the blueberry pie was on the house as we shirked out the door. I couldn't help feeling we had just crashed a party by claiming we were best friends with the host.

We finally saw Fortun with giant mountain cliffs jutting up on three sides, since this was the end of the long valley and the beginning of the fjord. The emerald water gave way to a thin strip of coast, where small wooden houses stood. Rock faces rose almost vertically for thousands of feet to peaks, where blue glaciers perched, offering streams of melting ice. The sun peeked over the precipice to spread its rays on the fertile valley and warm the three of us. Waterfalls plunged off cliffs like misty wedding veils shrouding the black rock. This one view of the fjord was more dramatic than any sight in Minnesota. Why would anyone leave? And if they did, wouldn't they miss this beauty?

Upon arrival, a feeling of panic set in because I had no plan for what we'd do here in Fortun other than snap a couple of photos to show folks back home. I didn't know anyone who lived here, since the remaining Drægni relatives had moved to northern Norway. I didn't know what we were here to discover.

We checked in to the Skjolden Hotel a few kilometers before Fortun, and the receptionist asked me, "You are Eric Dregni? You have guests for dinner this evening who will be coming at 5:30. We have been expecting you." Taken aback that anyone knew we were coming, Katy and I looked at each other anxiously.

At suppertime, a self-assured older woman with blonde-gray hair and a hand-knit sweater arrived hauling a giant book about the history of the town. "*God dag,* I'm Ingeborg. Your father's cousin Magne Drægni from Bodø called and asked me to meet you here." She sat down and opened up the heavy tome, which listed nearly everyone who had ever lived in the area.

In Ingeborg's book about the families from Fortun, she found my great-great-grandfather. "He took the name Drægni when he moved to that farm," she said, pointing up to a little ridge. Norway is full of hills, so they have many specific words for them like the Eskimos have for snow.

I told her about our meeting with Ole Berger Drægni in Turtagrø and that he said we're not related. She said that was true but added, "You are probably family one way or another. Everyone here is related somehow."

Ingeborg consulted her book again and informed me, "You should really be a Bolstad." Bolstad? What kind of name was that? I wondered. "Bolstad is the area where he came from. Or else you could be Olson because your great-great-grandfather's first name was Ole." Since Minnesota is full of this name, the last thing I wanted was to be another "Olson."

Last names in the Lusterfjord were like addresses. "When your great-great-grandfather moved to the Drægni farm to become the blacksmith, he took the surname 'Drægni.'" So that was when we assumed the title of "tree-dragger."

"Your great-great-grandmother lived right over there," and she pointed out the window to the edge of the fjord. "Her name was 'Eide,' which is—how is it in English? An *'eide'* is a special kind of hill with water around it and sticks out from the mountain."

I didn't know anything about Ellef's parents, my great-great-grandparents, other than their names. Perhaps because of the lack of land in the Lusterfjord, my great-great-grandfather couldn't inherit the family land in Bolstad before his parents died.

Ellef probably left because he couldn't get any land and would have been a tenant farmer, living and working on the land of the rich Drægni family and paying them much of his earnings. Not until 1928 did Norway abolish the tenant farmer system and allow the farmers to claim the land on which they lived. Because most of the land in Norway is rocks and glaciers, any patch of decent land was valuable.

Even though Norway is now the richest country in Europe with vast resources of oil, natural gas, and hydroelectric power, the area around Fortun struggles. I asked Ingeborg what her family grew on her farm. "Grass. We grow grass." In typical Norwegian fashion, she downplayed their beautiful berries and healthy farm animals.

Making a living off this little bit of land was nearly impossible in my great-grandfather's time because the relatively large population in this area shared the land. "Now there are about two hundred people here in Fortun, but before that there were ten times that number," Ingeborg said. "You can't eat beauty."

The next day, Ingeborg picked us up from the hotel to bring us to a *hytte* where we could spend the night. We would realize our dream of staying in a rugged cabin with a grass roof. Ingeborg's son had made the *hytte*, pulling the sod up by a rope to place on the roof.

Almost all the houses in the area are wedged on a tiny finger of shoreline between the water and the cliffs that rise up hundreds of feet. Occasionally, large houses are stuck halfway up the mountain with no visible road and only steep paths to reach the front door. Local legend tells of people who live up on the fjell next to the fjords who have to tie their kids to a leash so they don't fall off the cliffs at the edge of the yard.

Another tale Ingeborg told us was about the town of Stigen, on one of the branches of the Sognefjord, where some of the houses could be reached only by ladder. When the taxman came, people lifted the ladder and couldn't be taxed. Coming from flat Minnesota, I saw these mountains as obstacles, but Norwegians regarded them as safety. Or as the poet Wergeland wrote, "*Norges beste vern og feste er dets gamle fjell*" (Norway's best protection and security are its ancient peaks).

Although the mountains were stunning, I found the vertical cliffs claustrophobic. Ingeborg thought this was ironic because she and some friends went on a "Lusterfjord tour to North Dakota, Minnesota, and Wisconsin. We heard that many Norwegians who went to North Dakota got very sick there. They had some illness — how do you say — homesick? They were depressed and needed mountains to live." Ingeborg explained that Norwegians have an expression to explain this phenomenon, "*å være på vidda*" (to be in the high plains), which means to be crazy, lost, or simply in the wrong place.

I remember *Giants in the Earth*, by Ole Rölvaag, in which he described the slow insanity of life on the plains: "But more to be dreaded . . . was the strange spell of sadness which the unbroken solitude cast upon the minds of some. Many took their own lives; asylum after asylum was filled with disordered beings who had once been human. It is hard for the eye to wander from sky line to sky line, year in and year out, without finding a resting place!"

In fact, Johannes Drægni, the brother of great-grandfather Ellef, returned from Minnesota after a few years because he was homesick and unmarried and longed for the mountains.

Johannes abandoned his large raspberry farm in suburban Minneapolis — where Knollwood Plaza shopping center now stands — and returned to Luster. "Oh yes, I knew Johannes," Ingeborg told me. "He liked to show how successful he was in America, but he came back because of the lure of Norway, his country." My father, on the other hand, gave me the impression that Johannes was the brother who was something of a failure in Minnesota. Ingeborg insinuated that Johannes liked to flaunt his New World wealth: "When he came back to Fortun, he had much money and bought a farm. He didn't want to work, so his brother Martin worked the farm."

In the Lusterfjord, building on valuable farmland is frowned upon. One of the midwives for Eilif's birth who had worked in this area told us, "Along the Lusterfjord, they all have small houses because the fjell comes down. Boom!" She made a cutting motion with her hand. "Then the fjord begins with only a little bit of land in between. If people use all that land to build big houses, they have no room to grow anything. That's when other people get angry with them."

Although Fortun appeared prominently on maps of Norway, the town consists of a few houses, one tiny store, a school with a *barnehage* (day care), and a white church, which stood in stark contrast to the greenery and rock cliffs. This church was built for the town of Fortun in exchange for its Fantoft Stave Church that dated back to 1150 when the Vikings were being converted to Christianity. The local myths tell that the famous Viking builders transferred their ship-building skills to erecting stave churches, which were essentially upside-down boats. The carpenters kept the pagan dragons from the ships' bows and adorned the churches' eaves, much as Notre Dame has its menacing gargoyles. The Fantoft Stave Church of Fortun was moved to Bergen in 1883, and Ellef followed its path ten years later. The church was burned down in 1992 by a Satanist who called himself "The Count." The classic stave church, in which Ellef was probably baptized, has since been reconstructed in Bergen.

Next to the newer, white church, I recognized the grave-yard where my brothers and I played "war" as a child. Katy, Eilif, and I wandered through the moss-covered tombstones and discovered the tombstone of Ellef's mother, Karen J. Drægni, née Eide, born 11 July 1853, died 25 June 1921. Once Ellef left Fortun, he never saw his mother again. Now here we stood with his great-great-grandchild with the same name: the old Ellef who was born here and is buried in Minneapolis and the baby Eilif who came to Norway to be born. What journey will our son make?

Next to the church, a large sign pointed across the small river to "DRÆGNI." We could see the large family villa that belonged to the landowners and a few abandoned hovels around the field. We walked over the bridge and found a small shack next to the river on the site where Ellef's family house stood before it was carried off by high water.

I told Ingeborg that I had heard that my great-grand-father's house had flooded. She looked surprised. "That was just one of them," she said, and Katy and I were excited that perhaps his house was still intact somewhere. Then Ingeborg continued, "Another house he lived in had a big rock fall on it from the fjell and crush it."

Startled, I looked up at the cliffs and realized that beauty comes at a price. Driving to Ingeborg's *hytte* where we would be staying, she told us, "It is very common for rocks to fall in the summer, and then there can be avalanches in the winter." As we pulled into her dirt driveway, Katy and I were instantly enchanted by the log cabin's grass roof blooming with flowers. We sat on the porch of the cozy *hytte*, and Ingeborg pointed out a massive boulder in a field. "That rock came down last summer into our raspberry patch. We looked out, and there it was." Our thrill of staying in a classic cabin in my great-grandfather's hometown with our new baby was clouded when we walked out into the small field next to the house to look at the twelve-foot-high boulder. The stone sank two feet into the ground, and a half-foot-deep crater of earth made by the impact surrounded it. When the boulder had plummeted down, smaller, but still immovable, stones had broken off as a sort of cluster bomb to knock over many raspberry plants. "There is no way to move it, so we just farm around it," Ingeborg said.

It sounded like the myth of Sisyphus condemned to forever push a rock up a hill, only this time the rocks were raining, and chances were one might hit someone someday. My great-grandfather was probably wise to escape Norway while he still could and before he was crushed. Ingeborg wasn't concerned about the falling rocks because she loved the rugged landscape. "Any place you live has its dangers," she advised. I convinced myself that riding on the ferry in the fjord was surely more dangerous than sleeping under an impending rock slide. Still, it wasn't encouraging to see many of the small houses in the valley abandoned.

Just up the road, I recognized the house that belonged to Ola and Lina Drægni where I fell into the manure pile more than thirty years ago. Ola and Lina had passed away years before, and now their son Magne Drægni and his family would come down every year from Bodø for a summer vacation. Ingeborg had the key to the house because she took care of the property while everyone was away. "Magne told us to go inside to look at old family albums," she said as she wiggled the key in the lock.

Ingeborg pushed open the heavy wooden door, and our nostrils were filled with the scent of mothballs, which kept pests from aging the memories stored inside. Hand-stitched embroideries, teacups, and showcase glasses were displayed on decorative wooden shelves. Framed photos of Magne's family filled the space between.

Ingeborg led us up creaky stairs into the open loft to find the old albums. We ducked our heads down in the garret as Ingeborg looked for the lights. She flipped the switch, and bulbs illuminated family heirlooms. Hand-carved and painted bowls were hung from hooks, and a collection of silver spoons hung from a wooden rack. Ingeborg explained that when Ellef left, the fjord area was among the most destitute regions of Norway. People didn't use plates until the early 1900s, but used carved wooden boards or homemade flat bread to hold the food. Forks, on the other hand, had made it to the Lusterfjord by the 1850s. A large family porridge bowl now gathered dust but was once the focal point of the dinner table. Ellef's mother, Karen, whose grave we saw earlier in the day, served the evening *grøt* from this giant wooden bowl.

Then I noticed in the corner a clunky wooden chest that was the twin sister of Ellef's chest he carried to America. No "Halifax" sticker adorned the side, but the same simple hand-crafted latches kept the box shut tight. This must have been the chest that Johannes carried back from America. I slowly lifted the lid to find stacks of photo albums with decorative puffy covers, which added pomp to the black-and-white photos. The books' jackets were worn purple velvet, the color of royalty, as if to hide their humble background.

Ingeborg reached inside to pull out these archives of old photos and correspondence from Ellef and other relatives who left Norway. After all these years, the old documents were still preserved, and I had to travel back to this remote little town to uncover evidence of my great-grandfather. The old "Amerika letters," or rather postcards, from my great-grandfather Ellef and his sister Severina were sent back to people in Fortun from Minnesota. The text on the postcards was frustratingly sparse: "*Hilsen fra Amerika!*" (Greetings from America!). I was hoping to dig deeper into the mind of Ellef and his brave journey to an unknown world, but he kept his words to himself. I found a paragraph of Ellef's handwriting on the back of one of the postcards and thought it would finally shed some light on his story. Ingeborg studied the old text and translated. It said the weather in Minnesota was a bit chilly, but they were doing fine.

Ingeborg brought the photo albums out into the gentle sunshine beaming over the fjells. We sat on her patio and paged through the books as we listened to the water constantly plunging off the top of the mountain to the stream hundreds of feet below. And hoped no rocks were falling.

Although she said you couldn't eat the beauty of the Lusterfjord, you could taste the fresh raspberries as big as golf balls covered in heavy cream. "These are the small ones," Ingeborg said as she served us heaping bowls of berries.

I pondered the photo of Ellef dressed in a conservative three-piece, pin-striped suit with his sister, Severina, topped by a gigantic brimmed hat, and their brother, Johannes, who eventually came home to Fortun. The serious expressions, so common in photos of the era, perhaps showed that they were hard workers and didn't clown around. The picture was taken in Chicago and sent home to Norway as photographic evidence that they had indeed prospered in the New World.

I stared at these photos of my great-grandfather that dated back more than one hundred years and had been preserved by his relatives in Norway who didn't brave the rugged Atlantic. I could understand now why people remained here while others, like Johannes, left only to come back and be saved by beauty. I was sure if Ellef were alive, he'd wonder why I was spending my time writing about him rather than working a steady job. I'd tell him that something is always sacrificed to follow your dreams. He knew this.

Acknowledgments

Our newfound friends and acquaintances in Norway showed us a new way of living. Special thanks to Knut Astrup Bull and Inger Brøger Bull, for all the great quotations; Charlie Dee; Vigdis Devik; Magne and Rigmor Drægni, the long-lost relatives; Ole Magnus and Lise Drægni; Aud Fjeld; Rachel Haug and Arild; Shannon Johansen; Juri from Genova; Arild Juul, for the great photos; Dale Licata and everyone at the International House at NTNU; Ken Luebbering; David Mauk, for enlightening me about Norwegian immigration to Minnesota; Serena Motta; Sissel Robbins; Kari Schei; Lisa Sethre-Hofstad and family, for showing us the new "normal"; Astrid and Marie Solberg; Solveig; Ingeborg Steig and family in the Lusterfjord; Sigrid Torblå and all the *jordmødre* at the Orkdal Sykehus; T.O.S.K. (Trondheim Skooter Klub) and their glorious Lambretta TVs; Joffe and Runa Urnes; Leif Maliks and Vigdis Vikhammer (what a great name!); Marcella Volta; and Arne, Trond Arild, and Oddbjørg Walhstrøm.

Friends back home encouraged us and put up with my Norwegian babble these past years. Thanks to Sasha Aslanian and Leif Larsen, for all the Norsk books; Jay Dregni; Nickle S. Hook; Odd Lovoll; Pieter Martin; PK McCarthy, for everything; Bob and Cheryl McCarthy; Patti McCarthy and family, for taking care of the little 'uns while I wrote; Jim and Judy Mundt; Todd Orjala, for being patient with the revisions; John "Italia" Perkins and his terrible, terrible songs; Carla Scharber and the class in Cambridge; Jaya Shoffner; Allison Skoberg, for pointing out the flyer for the Fulbright exchange to Trondheim and starting this whole mess; Myrna Smith; Meredith Sommers; Margaret Tehven and her relatives in Lofoten; Wes Timgren, for hooking us up with friends of friends; Wendy Thompson; and Patricia Weaver Francisco.

Hans Eisenbeis, Julie Caniglia, and Tom Bartel at *The Rake* gave me the space to show how to get paid to make babies. Other editors also printed parts of our Norwegian adventure, including Berit Hessen and Marianne Onsrud Jawanda at *The Norway Times* in New York, Chris Welsch and Kerri Westenberg at the *Star Tribune* in the Twin Cities, and Anna Befort at the magazine for the Sons of Norway, *The Viking*.

The creative writing department at the University of Minnesota helped me shape the manuscript and cut out the fat. My appreciation to the stars of the staff, faculty, and visitors: Kathleen Glasgow; Patricia Hampl; Garrison Keillor, for showing me the value of *Janteloven* in Minnesota; Tracy Kidder; Philip Lopate, for showing me that the present tense is passé; Julie Schumacher; Mimi Sprengnether; and especially Charlie Sugnet. Fellow students in the MFA program at the University of Minnesota put up with constant revisions of this neverending manuscript: Tara DaPra, Arvonne Fraser, Laura Flynn, Nicole Johns, Carla-Elaine Johnson, Emily Johnson, Mary Kettl, John Lurie, Jake Mohan, Mike Rollins, Alyson Sinclair, and many others.

I received extremely generous grants to write this book from organizations that believed in the process (even though I had nothing to show them until now). Fulbright sent us to Trondheim in search of serendipity; Torskeklubben gave a two-year fellowship to keep us alive while I was typing away (I already miss the cod and aquavit); and Sons of Norway helped out with the liberal King Olav V Norwegian-American Heritage Fund. *Takk skal du ha!*

Snakker Du Norsk?

barnehage	children's day-care center (literally, "children's garden")
barnetoget	children's parade
barnetran	children's cod liver oil
bjørn	bear
brodder	spikes that clamp on the bottom of shoes to prevent slipping on ice; crampons
bunad	formal Norwegian folk costumes that vary from region to region (plural, *bunader*)
drosje	taxi
fjell	mountain
fri oppdragelse	"free upbringing," referring to the theory that children should not be held back or scolded
gravlaks	cured salmon
Ha det bra!	Good-bye!
helsestasjon	clinic in the schools (literally, "health station")
hytte	a cabin or hut, often very remote
innsjø	lake (literally, "inland sea")
ja	yes
Janteloven	"Jante's Law," based on a fictional Norwegian town and given as the reason why Norwegians are so reserved
jordmor	midwife (literally, "earth mother"; plural, *jordmødre*)
julebord	a Christmas table and party
kjøtt	meat (pronounced halfway between "shut" and "shit")
kro	small restaurant

Loke	the trickster god in Norse mythology who was sometimes malicious (also spelled Loki)
midnattsol	midnight sun
midnattsolvind	midnight sun wind (believed to occur the day after seeing the midnight sun)
mørketid	the dark time in the Norwegian winter when the sun rarely rises above the horizon
nei	no
nissen	elves (or more correctly, pixies)
oljefondet	government-saved money from oil (literally, "oil fund")
Oy!	exclamation meaning "Oh!" or "Wow!"
pølse	wiener (plural, *pølser)*
Rådhuset	city hall
rakfisk	fermented fish (usually trout)
risegrøt	rice porridge
rorbu	fishermen's cabins, often on stilts over the water, especially in the Lofoten Islands
rosemaling	decorative Scandinavian painting (often on old chests, wooden beds, or tables)
russ	graduating high schoolers who play pranks
rømme	heavy sour cream with very high (35 percent) fat content (often put on waffles or used to make *rømmegrøt* porridge)
rømmegrøt	porridge made from *rømme* and flour, then smothered in butter (also *rømmegraut)*
samboer	couple living together but not married, with many of the same legal rights as those bound by wedlock
smørbrød	open-faced sandwich (literally, "butter bread")
spark	a stand-up kick sled
Storting	the Norwegian parliament in Oslo
sykehus	hospital (literally, "sick house")
syttende mai	seventeenth of May, Norwegian Constitution Day

takk	thanks
torsk	cod
tosk	fool (literally, "cod")
tran	cod liver oil
trolls	stupid monsters, often with many heads, who live in the wilderness and turn to stone if they see daylight
trygdekontor	public insurance office
Uff da!	exclamation meaning anything from "Ouch!" to "Oh!" (also *Huff dah*)

Eric Dregni is assistant professor of writing at Concordia University in St. Paul. He is the author of several books, including *Minnesota Marvels* (Minnesota, 2001) and *Midwest Marvels* (Minnesota, 2006).